WINSLOW HOMER
ILLUSTRATING AMERICA

WINSLOW HOMER
ILLUSTRATING AMERICA

Marilyn S. Kushner

Barbara Dayer Gallati

Linda S. Ferber

BROOKLYN MUSEUM OF ART
in association with
GEORGE BRAZILLER • PUBLISHER

First published in the United States of America in 2000 by
George Braziller, Inc.
171 Madison Avenue
New York, NY 10016

Library of Congress Cataloging-in-Publication Data:

Kushner, Marilyn S., 1948–
    Winslow Homer : illustrating America / Marilyn S.
Kushner, Barbara Dayer Gallati, Linda S. Ferber.
        p. cm.
    Includes bibliographical references.
    ISBN 0-8076-1466-1
    1. Homer, Winslow, 1836–1910—Catalogs. 2. United
States—In art—Catalogs. 3. Brooklyn Museum of Art—
Catalogs. I. Gallati, Barbara Dayer. II. Ferber, Linda S.
III. Title.

NE1112.H6 A4 2000
769.92—dc21   00-020003

Edited by Joanna Ekman

Designed by Rita Lascaro

Printed in Hong Kong

FIRST EDITION

ACKNOWLEDGMENTS

The Brooklyn Museum of Art celebrated a major gift from
the collector Harvey Isbitts by presenting the exhibition
Winslow Homer: Illustrating America from July to October
of 1999. The exhibition, organized by the three authors of
this volume—Marilyn S. Kushner, Curator of Prints and
Drawings; Barbara Dayer Gallati, Curator of American
Painting and Sculpture; and Linda S. Ferber, Andrew W.
Mellon Curator of American Art—provided the inspiration
for this book.

The curators are grateful to the following colleagues and
scholars for their advice: Philip C. Beam, Amy Beth, David
B. Dearinger, Abigail Booth Gerdts, William H. Gerdts,
Jonathan Harding, James O'Donnell, and David Tatham.
Other research assistance was contributed by Francesca
Bacci, Giovanella Brusatin, Elizabeth Christensen, Frances
Cohen, Holly Hatheway, Biljiana Kesic, Elysa Lipsky-
Karasz, Shirley Rabin, and Jodi Rodgers. At the Brooklyn
Museum of Art, the project benefited from the professional
contributions of many staff members, including Dean
Brown, Sarah Desantes, Joanna Ekman, Charles Froom,
Amy Gerbracht, Sarah Elizabeth Kelly, Elaine Komorowski,
Deirdre Lawrence, James Leggio, Barbara Head Millstein,
Antoinette Owen, Sarah Snook, and Gregg Stanger. Also to
be thanked is Norman Dubrow for his role in facilitating the
donation of the wood engravings to the Museum. Special
recognition must be given to Phyllis Kwalwasser, Stephanie
Leverock, and Dara Sicherman, three people at the Museum
whose assistance was integral to the success of this project.

For the ongoing support of the Museum's Trustees,
special gratitude must be extended to Robert S. Rubin,
Chairman, and every member of the Board. Without the
confidence and active engagement of the Trustees, it would
not be possible to initiate and maintain the high level of
exhibition and publication programming exemplified by
Winslow Homer: Illustrating America.

CONTENTS

FOREWORD

The Brooklyn Museum of Art's comprehensive collection of nineteenth-century American art includes not only many fine paintings and sculptures treasured by the public but, additionally, extensive holdings in the Department of Prints, Drawings, and Photographs, which help to tell a more complete story of the visual arts in the nineteenth century. We were, therefore, especially grateful when Harvey Isbitts generously donated his marvelous collection of more than two hundred fifty Winslow Homer wood-engraved illustrations to the Museum in 1998. The passionate care that Mr. Isbitts has given these works of art over the past twenty-five years was matched by his joy in turning his treasures into a public collection.

During Homer's career as an illustrator between 1857 and 1878, he created a body of works that are regarded today as among the finest wood-engraved illustrations of that century. As a commercial draftsman, he worked with master engravers in partnerships that created some of the most memorable illustrations of the period. In this volume, seventy-nine plates of engravings, with accompanying entries, are introduced by two essays: one, by Barbara Dayer Gallati, exploring Homer's iconography through an examination of the relation of his engravings to his oils and watercolors; and the other, by Marilyn S. Kushner, surveying the world of wood engraving and Homer's relationship with wood engravers of his time.

In organizing the book thematically rather than chronologically and reuniting the engravings with some of the original texts that accompanied them, Barbara Dayer Gallati, Marilyn S. Kushner, and Linda S. Ferber have set Winslow Homer's work in historical and social context. Like his contemporaries, the European Impressionists, Homer was an observer of modern life, but his images of nineteenth-century America should not be read literally. In fact, they were (like popular imagery today) subtle and convincing inventions that reflected and supported mainstream taste and widely held ideas about social values, gender roles, and class relations. Homer's keen eye for current events and social manners and mores set his images apart from more conventional magazine work and enabled him to create some of the most memorable illustrations of the time.

Arnold L. Lehman
Director
Brooklyn Museum of Art

Narrative Strategies in Winslow Homer's Art

Barbara Dayer Gallati

Winslow Homer's early career as a freelance illustrator is well documented, but owing to the subordinate position of illustration within artistic hierarchies, this aspect of his oeuvre is usually treated as a separate chapter in his life that is not recounted in artistic terms.[1] Only in rare instances are his wood engravings considered as more than mere comparative adjuncts in the process of determining the meaning of his paintings.[2] This essay contends that although Homer responded to these artistic hierarchies, the drawings he created for engraved reproduction in mass-circulation periodicals deserve greater attention, for deeper study of them will augment our understanding of Homer's iconography in the other "more important" mediums of oil and watercolor. In fact, although all of Homer's designs for wood engravings are generally lumped into the category of illustration, a number of them had no accompanying texts (or inspired the texts that did accompany them). Removed from their customary function of acting in tandem with editorial, reportorial, or fictional commentary, these images within Homer's freelance output do not truly qualify as illustration but stand on their own and thus demand further integration within Homer's work as a whole. The following discussion points to a few examples in which a more thorough examination of Homer's engravings sheds new light on the interpretation of his paintings and on the creative process by which the narrative content of his oils evolved.

Sharpshooter (fig. 1) marks a watershed in Winslow Homer's career in that it is the artist's first significant work in the oil medium.[3] The painting, dated 1863, was not exhibited until 1864, when it was shown at the Atheneum Club in New York City, drawing respectable critical commentary.[4] Yet, before the painting was displayed, the image itself—that of a Union sharpshooter perched in a tree taking aim at the enemy—had already been seen by thousands in a variant engraved form published as *The Army of the Potomac—A Sharp-Shooter on Picket Duty* in the November 15, 1862, issue of *Harper's Weekly* (pl. 26); the caption noted that the engraving was "From a Painting by W. Homer, Esq."[5] Without benefit of examining the painting and wood engraving together, it would be easy to miss the subtle differences between the two. The iconographic discrepancies, though few, are nevertheless meaningful and may be taken as interpretive guides in determining how Winslow Homer (1836–1910) negotiated the transition from popular illustrator to maker of high art, a fifteen-year process during which he experimented with images in watercolor and oil that frequently find parallels in his designs for wood engravings.

Homer conceived the sharpshooter illustration and oil painting simultaneously. One can imagine his careful deliberations as he considered the audiences for which each was fashioned. As one of the foremost illustrators of his time (even at this early stage in his career), he had learned the value and appeal that a

Fig. 1. Winslow Homer. *Sharpshooter,* 1863. Oil on canvas, 12¼ x 16½ inches (31.1 x 41.9 cm). 3.1993.3, Gift of Barbro and Bernard Osher, Portland Museum of Art, Maine

crisp, reportorial, action-filled image held for the readers of *Harper's,* the chief source of his income as a freelance artist from 1857 to 1875. Until 1863 the wood engravings that Homer designed were juxtaposed with editorials or articles to which they related, often specifically. The complementary relationship between picture and text generally conformed to the traditional balance whereby the image was put in service of the word to clarify or enlarge narrative meaning. A major disruption of this balance occurred, however, with the sharpshooter engraving. In it the nature of the pictorial effort becomes emblematic, and the overall reception of meaning relies not on the written word but on the viewer's ability to fathom content without an accompanying text. It should be noted that the illustrations by Johannes Adam Simon Oertel, Alfred R. Waud, and Thomas Nast contained in the same issue as the *Sharp-Shooter* (also relating to the maneuvers of the Army of the Potomac) did receive explanatory texts.[6]

Homer's consciousness of the delicate operation of narrative can be observed in the differences between the engraving and the painting. As pared down as its narrative is, the wood engraving still reveals its greater relationship to illustration: as compared with the figure in the painting, the sharpshooter's form is larger and closer to the picture plane. The soldier cuts a more graphically dynamic figure because the pine branches surrounding him are less luxuriant and thus allow the jagged contours of his body greater clarity against the foil of the sky. The formal language of the wood engraving, by its own nature, endows a sharpness to the image, reinforcing the cold brutality of the marksman's purpose, which Homer found "as near murder as anything [he] could think of in connection with the army."[7] Supposedly able to pick off his target from a mile distant, the sharpshooter takes on the role of predatory bird, secreted on high and aided by seemingly preternatural eyesight (abetted here by the newly perfected telescopic sight of the gun). As if to introduce the metaphor of the sharpshooter as a bird of prey, Homer or the engraver or both accentuated the face of the soldier, whose hard, angular features, aquiline nose, and steely, glinting eye give him a hawklike aspect. Although such associations are undeniably present in the painting, the brittle effects are moderated: the oil medium softens because of its capacity to evoke atmosphere; color automatically eliminates the effects of the harsh, reductive contrast of black and white; the face is more softly modeled and hence, less individualized; and the viewer is distanced from the soldier-subject because of compositional adjustments. In all, the effect of the painting is less brutal and, consequently, less charged with narrative potential. The differences cited here might initially be attributed merely to the demands of wood engraving—the need to create an effective image from a strictly linear formal language expressed in black and white. However, the canteen hanging prominently on the tree at the right in the engraving provides strong evidence in the argument for Homer's deliberate insertion of a hint of narrative interplay in the *Harper's* image. The canteen interjects a sense of duration of time extending beyond the moment of taking aim for the fatal shot; the detail thus promotes a narrative process in the viewer, who is prompted to imagine the marksman's long hours spent sitting in wait. What is more, the targetlike shape of the canteen realigns the viewer's attention, subliminally suggesting the human target that exists outside the pictorial space.[8]

Iconographic readings such as the ones outlined here are admittedly subjective, but the fact that Homer modified the sharpshooter motif in these ways suggests that his choices were rooted in an objective. One possible objective might have been to promote his budding career as a painter through his widely reproduced wood engravings by making those designs more like the paintings he was beginning to exhibit.[9] Such an explanation would account for the occasional (and, as time passed, more frequent) elision of anecdotal vignettes from his illustrations in favor of motifs of greater formal and dramatic power. Not only did such a practice of simplifying and abstracting a larger idea from a welter of detail strengthen the effectiveness of Homer's illustrations aesthetically and separate them qualitatively from the work of other illustrators, but it also lessened the division between illustration and "high art" painting at a time when gravity (or complexity) of subject was hierarchically regulated according to the medium in which it was presented. Thus, although Homer's tendency to deactivate the narrative is shown in both sharpshooter images, it is the oil (the medium of high art) that conveys the least narrative information. Despite his lack of formal training, Homer's awareness of the academic ranking of art by medium—drawing, watercolor, and oil, in ascending order of importance—and the limitations controlling function and subject matter appropriate to each must be assumed, for such issues were commonly debated among the artists of his generation. The connections between the artist's illustrations, watercolors, and oils created up to 1875 demand exploration in the light of the hierarchical relationships linking medium and subject. This essay offers a set of introductory examples that reveal the artist's adherence to established expectations with respect to the role of narrative in illustration and high art.

The evolution of the croquet theme in Homer's work offers another illuminating case. The artist's wood engravings of this subject and others testify that he had, in many ways, already qualified as a chronicler (if not painter) of modern life well before Charles Baudelaire's writings containing that potent concept became current in the United States.[10] Yet, despite the topical nature of his drawings for *Harper's* and other magazines, they were (with the exception of his Civil War images) rarely the products of direct observation. Rather, he would often rely on a collection of stock figures or motifs from his repertoire, moving them from composition to composition like pieces on a chessboard. The most familiar of these figures is a fashionable young woman, seen in profile, who leans either on her parasol, walking stick, or croquet mallet, depending on the context in which she is placed. She takes prominence at the right of Homer's enigmatic oil *Croquet Match* of 1868–69 (fig. 2), in which her isolation from the five other women in the painting suggests emotional tension and opposition—the meaning of which remains to be addressed in Homer literature. Homer's repeated use of this figure cannot be attributed to artistic laziness or lack of imagination. The iconic form transcends superficial storytelling and, in its repetition, cumulatively takes on a symbolic function. Seen in this way, this anonymous figure (usually her head is so radically profiled that her facial expression is unseen) deserves consideration as a sign of modern womanhood standing on the brink of change. Her posture denotes impatient anticipation and implies forward movement, but her feet, rooted to the ground, betray that her progress (whether in a game of croquet or perhaps in the larger game of life) is at a momentary standstill.

The validity of such an interpretation is impossible to establish, for Homer was adamant in maintaining silence about the content of his art as well as his private life. A number of factors, however, help to substantiate the belief that the artist was sensitive to the changing status of women in society, not the least of which is the fact that women were often the pivotal characters in his depictions of American life. His graphic art encompassed their roles "at home," during the war, their entry into the labor force, and their social interactions with and without men. The writings of his close associate, the artist-writer Eugene

Fig. 2. Winslow Homer. *Croquet Match,* 1868–69. Oil on millboard, 9³⁄₁₆ x 15⅝ inches (23.2 x 39.7 cm). 1999.72, Terra Foundation for the Arts, Daniel J. Terra Collection. Photograph courtesy of Terra Museum of American Art, Chicago

Benson (1839–1908), whose essay "The 'Woman Question'" was published in the December 15, 1866, *Galaxy,* are relevant to Homer's own treatment of the subject.[11] Well versed in contemporary French art (he also wrote about Jean-Léon Gérôme and Eugène Fromentin, among other French painters), Benson is a likely source to whom we may look for additional understanding of Homer's art of the 1860s and early 1870s. Although their relationship demands a study in itself, it must suffice here to point out that the two occupied studios in the University Building at the same time; Benson, the art critic for the *New York Evening Post* writing as "Sordello," was the most vocal advocate of Homer's early paintings; and the works of the two were shown together for a studio-clearing sale in November 1866.[12] These connections suggest a more than casual relationship between the two men, or at least allow us to presume an active exchange of ideas between them on the subject of their art.[13]

The relevance of Benson's essay about the "woman question" (which took the form of a series of general observations on types of women) is not necessarily related to Homer's iconography, but it is an indicator of the practice of typological categorizing that prevailed in the nineteenth century. A similar means of organizing content is revealed explicitly in Homer's illustrations that depend on the viewer's recognition of specific types of women—country girl, laborer, fashion plate, debutante, or, in the context of this discussion, the restless young woman on the right in *Croquet Match,* who may be read as a sign of modernity. This emblematic figure appears again in two 1869 wood engravings showing young women playing croquet, *Summer in the Country* and *What Shall We Do Next?* (pls. 46, 47), and the heightened narrative elements of those engraved illustrations may provide a key to the painting's meaning.

As David Park Curry has pointed out in his fascinating study of Homer's series of five paintings devoted to the croquet theme executed from 1865 to about 1869, the symbolism attached to the game itself was fraught with sexual innuendo readily understood by the nineteenth-century audience.[14] The article about croquet that appeared directly below *Summer in the Country* in *Appletons' Journal of Literature, Science and Art* explained the social implications of the game:

> *It has, indeed, been wickedly intimated that the real popularity of croquet is derived from another cause. There is more or less flirtation connected with the game, it is believed, and the admirable opportunities it offers for little coquettish comedies are supposed to have largely to do with the favor the sport enjoys. Acquaintance ripens readily under its auspices; there are the side-whispers, the banterings, the number less coquetries, the rivalry on the one hand, and the copartnership on the other, the merry-making that youth and good spirits call up; and hence young men and women find the sport highly conducive to that keener and subtler game that youth and beauty are always eager to play.*[15]

Curiously, the girls in *Summer in the Country* and in *What Shall We Do Next?* fail to match the vision of "Arcadian content" thought to be the product of hours spent at the game in "the sunshine and grass, and the flowers and the soft, refreshing airs, and the peaceful quiet," according to the *Appletons'* article. In place of conviviality and communal enjoyment, we find psychological intensity generated possibly by the competitive, strategic nature of the game. If, as Curry proposes, croquet imagery was replete with metaphors concerning the politics of social interaction between the sexes, then Homer's images of women playing without male company can also be interpreted in that way—as subtle references to the politics among women negotiating new social territory. In this light, not only does the playful caption "What Shall We Do Next?" take on a larger meaning, providing narrative information indicating that the game has reached a critical point demanding revised strategies, but it also suggests that American women as a whole must reassess their position in society. This meaning attains clarity through Homer's division of the composition, which literally places the young women in different spheres: the citified fashion plates playing the game occupy the lawn and thus are positioned outside the traditional domestic domain, while the three on the porch remain within the sheltered precinct of home (and traditional homely values). Yet even among the three homebodies differences emerge. The oldest of them ignores the spectacle of modernity before her, keeping her eyes to her sewing as she sits erect in her straight-back chair. The purity of her profile, the clean lines of her simple clothing, and the symmetry of her pose evoke a classicizing sensibility that embraces the ideal of tradition. The younger two, however, stand at the threshold (the edge of the porch) dividing both spheres, and they seem nonplussed, undecided as to whether they should join the game or remain in familiar and predictable regions. As adolescents, they stand at another threshold, at the brink of maturity and the concomitant independence of decision making. In this way as well, Homer focuses on choices facing women in post–Civil War America.

The compositional similarities displayed in *Croquet Match* and *What Shall We Do Next?* are so strong that they scarcely require describing. The veranda functions similarly in each as a type of liminal social space, with comparable dramas seeming to take place among the women and girls. In *Croquet Match* the "modern" woman looks outward, away from the porch; a "transitional" figure hugs the post but looks toward the lawn as if tempted to step down and play; and another, seated in a wooden folding chair, looks down at the shuttlecock in her lap. A battledore rests against the side of her chair. These, the three major protagonists, are observed from a slight distance by a cluster of three women, all dressed in white and possessing no individualized attributes, apart from the fact that each one's gaze is directed to a different woman in the principal group. The women of this tightly composed trio may be the local gossips, but given the theatrical tensions of the scene, they may also be likened to a Greek chorus. The drama that they witness, however, takes on a level of narrative ambiguity that Homer may have deemed appropriate for a painting. A second iconic figure— the seated woman—balances the figure on the right by providing the thematic and compositional oppositions on which Homer so often relied. In this and other contexts in which this motif appears, the seated woman seems to represent nostalgic, poetic, or romantic meaning. She, too, is isolated—if not physically, then psychologically. Like her "sister" in *What Shall We Do Next?*, this woman is emotionally removed from the situation, here for reasons hinted at by her identification with another game, battledore and shuttlecock, an old-fashioned children's or women's amusement that was usually played alone or sometimes with another.[16] A telltale scrap of paper lies on the porch. The bright white of the paper brings to this small detail an odd prominence and suggests its thematic weight in the narrative that Homer seems to spin, opening questions about the possible failure of a lover to appear for an assignation (hence the dejected posture of the seated woman and the untouched racket and shuttle-cock, which may symbolize her lonely status), or perhaps a romantic triangle. Homer used the motif of this seated figure in a contemporaneous drawing, *Waiting for Calls on New-Year's Day* (pl. 45), a work from *Harper's Bazar* that highlights the social tradition among women to conduct open houses on New Year's Day, when they eagerly awaited gentlemen callers.[17] Although the raison d'être of the image is clear, Homer inserts an anomalous element through the only seated woman, who, despite her position at the center foreground of the composition, assumes the same posture of resignation as her counterpart in *Croquet Match.* This sensibility is underscored by other compositional and stylistic features: she is the only figure who does not turn to the window expec-tantly, and she does not match the other women in terms of figure type or style of dress. What is more, her simplicity is emphasized by the comparative rustic-ity of her wooden folding chair, which seems so out of place among the other-wise plush furnishings in this formal parlor. The lingering air of disappointment surrounding this solitary figure is accented by the discarded flower that rests on the open expanse of floor behind her, operating in much the same way as the

Fig. 3. Winslow Homer. *Portrait of Helena de Kay,* circa 1873. Oil on panel, 12¼ x 18½ inches (31 x 47 cm). © Museo Thyssen-Bornemisza, Madrid

scrap of paper on the country veranda by suggesting that she, too, has been dis-appointed or discarded. This motif prefigures Homer's startlingly spare *Portrait of Helena de Kay* of circa 1873 (fig. 3), a painting that has perplexed art histori-ans in their efforts to extract from it a tale of romance between the artist and his sitter.[18] The mystery of Homer's romantic life aside, it is reasonable to speculate that his choice of the already established motif (carrying the meaning of nostalgia and rejection) for the de Kay portrait held specific meaning for him.

As seen in the case of *Croquet Match,* the discovery of content in Homer's paintings is often facilitated by examining his related wood engravings, wherein the visual narrative dimension is stronger. In cases when poems or prose texts accompanied the engravings, they provided the reader an additional narrative source, regardless of whether or not the image inspired or was inspired by those texts.[19] In some instances, the joining of picture and text brings greater clarity to

Fig. 4. Winslow Homer. *The Noon Recess,* 1873. Oil on canvas, 9¼ x 14⅛ inches (23.5 x 35.9 cm). The Warner Collection of Gulf States Paper Corporation, Tuscaloosa, Alabama

the content of a related work in oil. This is especially true in connection with *The Noon Recess* (fig. 4). The painted and engraved versions of this image vary only slightly, but enough so to suggest that the engraved form (pl. 52) was modified by Homer to suit the *Harper's Weekly* audience, which perhaps was less adept at reckoning the full meaning of the image without the additional visual clues. Commonly observed differences between the painted and engraved versions include details in the engraving that are absent in the painting: the map of North America on the wall that forms a backdrop for the daydreaming schoolteacher, and the notations on the blackboard behind the child that display the artist's witty self-references (his initials and the letters of the alphabet from *A* to *H*).[20] A further variation, which does not seem to have been noticed previously, is the glimpse of young girls at play outside the window at the left of the composition. In the painting, only the boy's detention is contrasted by the view of his male schoolmates through the open window next to the blackboard. By inserting the little girls at recess, Homer subtly charged the narrative line that focuses on the teacher's situation by shifting from the idea of child's play to adult desire.[21] This reading is confirmed by the poem, the last stanza of which addresses the young schoolmistress: "Ah! Weary one, whose brain is filled / With tiresome sounds the livelong day, / E'en now, your heart doth half incline / To let the captive out to play; / For yonder some one waits for you: / Shall love, or duty, find you true?" Both the oil and the engraving were done in 1873, making it likely that the creation of the two overlapped; but as in the case of the engraving and painting of the sharpshooter, the oil was less obvious in its delivery of content.

In the case of the engraving *The Morning Bell* (pl. 53), the chronology of image and text is complicated by the likelihood that Homer's 1871 oil, origi-

Fig. 5. Winslow Homer. *The Old Mill* (also known as *The Mill* and *The Morning Bell*), 1871. Oil on canvas, 24 x 38¼ inches (61 x 97.2 cm). Bequest of Stephen Carlton Clark, B.A. 1903, Yale University Art Gallery

nally titled *The Old Mill* (fig. 5), inspired the poem called "Morning Bell," which, in turn, prompted *Harper's* to commission the 1873 wood engraving.[22] As Nicolai Cikovsky, Jr., has argued, the painting's content appears to refer to the changing conditions of factory labor in New England. His reading of the painting rests on the premise that the young worker crosses a bridge that takes her beyond the mill to a new factory, which we cannot see. Her new, brightly colored clothing evidences her participation in a new economic order, which permits her to purchase goods; what is more, Cikovsky links this central figure with immigrant populations new to the American workforce and contrasts her with the group of girls, at the right, who may just be starting their "careers" in the factory. In distinguishing the different contents of the two versions,

Cikovsky concludes: "*Old Mill,* to use a word coined at about the time it was painted, is about the sociology of modern industrial change; *The Morning Bell,* about the subject of modern industrial time."[23]

Although Cikovsky's interpretation of *The Old Mill* and its divergence from *The Morning Bell* may provide insight into Homer's original intent, his ideas are grounded in the hypothetical. Moreover, as Cikovsky himself points out, at least one critic who saw the painting at the 1872 exhibition at the National Academy of Design mistook the mill for an old schoolhouse, a fact indicative of the common resistance of much of Homer's painted imagery to easy narrative exposition.[24] No such mistakes can be made, however, in the reading of the engraving. This version of the composition makes an immediate and firm connection between the title and the vigorous sounding of the bell (which is more prominently rendered in this instance). All of the figures wear the same kind of homespun clothing, and instead of creating a contrast between types of women working in factories, the engraving emphasizes the literal and figurative progression of workers in the labor force, starting with men, boys, and finally women, who were newcomers in this territory. Like the porch in other Homer compositions, the bridge to the old mill (or the new factory) registers as yet another type of liminal, transitional space for women as they cross the social threshold from domestic to industrial work. Homer's routine of bringing his figures closer to the picture plane in compositions destined for engraving is also evident here. This practice of "enlarging" further aligned the images with illustrations and thus encouraged the reader-viewer to seek a story line. Ironically, the story line of "modern industrial time" that Cikovsky constructed for the engraving finds its best proof in iconography that he did not fully explore—the motif of the two women in the right foreground. The pair's key position is blatantly signaled by the direct, outward gaze of the younger woman. The duo (roughly comparable to the small group gathered at the right in *The Old Mill*) calls to mind the familiar theme of youth and old age and, tied with the closing lines of the poem accompanying the engraving ("And so the morning bell rings ever on, / And so the weary feet obey its call, / Till o'er the earth silence at last shall come, / And death bring peace and rest alike to all"), reveals the ultimate subject: the deadening workaday tedium associated with factory life.[25] The bell signals the start of days that would inevitably blur into years. Yes, this engraving has to do with industrial time, but perhaps not as specifically or exclusively as Cikovsky proposes and not by the route of indirect evidence that he presents so logically. Instead, meaning is determined by the evidence presented by Homer himself. In that connection, it is useful to examine Homer's earlier (1868) engraving, *New England Factory Life—"Bell-Time"* (fig. 6), in which he also included a youth–old age motif at the right of the composition. That Homer intended the viewer to draw particular meaning from this grouping of a wan young woman

NEW ENGLAND FACTORY LIFE—"BELL-TIME."—DRAWN BY WINSLOW HOMER.—[SEE PAGE 471.]

Fig. 6. Winslow Homer. *New England Factory Life—"Bell-Time,"* from *Harper's Weekly,* July 25, 1868, p. 472. Wood engraving, 9¾ x 14 inches (24.8 x 35.6 cm). Art Reference Library, Brooklyn Museum of Art

and her haggard older companion is obvious. Their faces, which verge on caricature to enhance expressive potential, emerge from the crowd as vivid, white, unhatched areas. The older woman bends forward, gesturing as if to urge the other to quicken her step toward a goal that will further exhaust and age her. A young woman at the far left also takes on special relevance in this context, for she too stands out as a unique face in the crowd. Alert and erect, she may be identified as a foreshadowing of the central figure in *The Old Mill* and offers a clear contrast in type to her compositional counterpart on the right. Again, in this Homeric conjunction of opposites, a kernel of meaning leading to the content of *The Old Mill* is discovered in this young woman, who has adjusted to the new regulations of factory life and profits by them.

This reading of Homer's iconographic development along the theme of the increased female presence in industrialized labor depends on three works—the 1868 *New England Factory Life* engraving, the 1871 *Old Mill* painting, and the 1873 *Morning Bell* engraving—and suggests once more how one of Homer's major oils was distilled from thematic and compositional devices that he had already put to good use in an earlier engraving. In this instance the 1868 engraving embraced both of the ideas that Cikovsky found so distinctly rendered in *The Old Mill* and *The Morning Bell,* and the two themes may be interpreted as variations on a set of ideas that had concerned Homer for nearly six years.

Homer's quest for a place in the profession of the higher art of oil painting was a risky endeavor for him, certainly financially, and probably psychologically. As his exhibition activity increased in New York (at such venues as the National Academy of Design, the Artists' Fund Society, the American Watercolor Society, and the Century Association) and his paintings gained respect among his colleagues (as witnessed by his election to full academician at the National Academy in 1865), he continued to pour considerable energy into his freelance work, supplying images for magazines and books. Although his eagerness to escape what he considered the drudgery of such commissions is often cited (and no doubt true), his delay in severing his business associations with publishers seems to have rested not only on financial matters but also on the fact that his own identity as an artist was promoted by his widely circulated wood engravings. Linda S. Ferber has

noted elsewhere in this volume that, even in his early designs, "Homer's emergence as an independent talent is charted by the evolution of his signature in the *Ballou's* series from 'W. H.' to 'Homer' to mention in texts as 'Our artist, Mr. Homer.'"[26] Homer's desire to assert his personality through his art is revealed in the inventive ways he sometimes devised to mark his authorship of the engravings. The most obvious and delightful of these is found in *The Beach at Long Branch* (pl. 65), in which a charming young woman appears to have just completed inscribing Homer's initials in the sand. By signing in this manner, Homer not only became part of the image but also encouraged viewers to seek him out in much the same way that Alfred Hitchcock teased movie audiences to detect him in a second or two of footage on the screen. At times Homer's placement of his name or initials in the composition also helps the viewer to locate the crux of his

Fig. 7. Winslow Homer. *The Dinner Horn*, 1870. Oil on canvas, 19¼ x 13¾ inches (48.9 x 34.9 cm). 1994.59.2, Collection of Mr. and Mrs. Paul Mellon, © 1999 Board of Trustees, National Gallery of Art, Washington, D.C.

ironic humor. This is particularly true of *The Dinner Horn* (pl. 48), in which his initials appear inscribed in the basin at the lower left. As if to mark the playful parallels between the attractions of the noonday meal and those of the sturdy young woman who sounds the call, Homer's initials form a triangle with the girl's neatly turned ankles and the desirous gaze of the cat to evoke a comically suggestive meaning. This engraving appeared in *Harper's Weekly* in June 1870, the same year that Homer painted the first of three closely related canvases featuring the same robust figure blowing the dinner horn (but eliminating the slyly humorous narrative provided by the cat) (fig. 7). It may be surmised that, because of the engraving's fully elaborated composition and content, and because it appeared early in that year, Homer's work on the engraving coincided with his work on the first oil. This conjunction suggests that Homer again deliberately "debuted" a painting in the form of an engraving (which emphatically

Fig. 8. Winslow Homer. *Waiting for a Bite* (probably originally *Why Don't the Suckers Bite?*), circa 1874. Watercolor and graphite on wove paper, 7 5/16 x 13 5/16 inches (18.7 x 34 cm). 1948.28, gift of Mary D. and Arthur Williston, © Addison Gallery of American Art, Phillips Academy, Andover, Massachusetts, all rights reserved

declared his identity through his "signature" humor) and thereby prepared an audience to welcome the less narratively explicit oil in the event of its display.[27]

Homer seems to have applied similar tactics with respect to his watercolors, as if to exploit the recognition that he had achieved among the larger audience for popular imagery to prepare a market for his art. A case in point is the chronology of a suite of three works concentrating on the same motif of a group of boys fishing on an Adirondack lake: the engraving *Waiting for a Bite* (pl. 18), which was published in the August 22, 1874, issue of *Harper's Weekly;* the watercolor now known by the same title, but probably originally *Why Don't the Suckers Bite?* (fig. 8); and the oil, *Waiting for a Bite* (fig. 9). It makes no difference in this instance as to which came first, for all three date roughly to 1874, indicating Homer's simultaneous involvement with the motif in the three mediums. What does obtain here, however, is that the engraving appeared first in a context that implied its role as illustration. Thus, despite the fact that there was no text relating to it, the engraving would have assumed a narrative identity because of where it was seen. The watercolor, on the other hand, was one of thirteen by Homer that were exhibited in February 1875 at the Eighth Annual Exhibition of the American Society of Painters in Watercolor (later the American Watercolor Society). Listed as no. 71 in the catalogue, it was for sale for fifty dollars (approximately the same amount that Harper Brothers had paid him ten years earlier for a large drawing).[28] The sum set for the watercolor is a potent reminder of the still relatively lowly rank of watercolor painting at that time and the fact that its popularity (and, indeed, the momentum of the watercolor movement itself) was

Fig. 9. Winslow Homer. *Waiting for a Bite,* 1874. Oil on canvas, 12 x 20 inches (30.5 x 50.8 cm). C.O.119.1, Bequest of Ninah May Cummer, The Cummer Museum of Art and Gardens, Jacksonville, Florida

largely a result of the affordability of these "inconsequential" sheets of paper, which, in the opinion of some critics, were little more than colored drawings.[29]

Homer's recognition of watercolor's interstitial position—it was virtually the bridge between illustration and oil painting—might also be reflected in his choice of childhood imagery as the dominant subject matter of his first notable bids for attention as a watercolorist. As a medium considered "too weak" to sustain high-minded, challenging subject matter, watercolor lent itself well to Homer's childhood themes, nostalgic evocations of endless summer days. Helen Cooper has observed that Homer's choice of childhood imagery suited his need for innovative subjects and meshed with the growing trend in American literature (exemplified in works of Mark Twain and Louisa May Alcott) to focus on themes involving young people.[30] Homer's experience illustrating children's literature and poetry about childhood indicates that, although the subject matter was not new to his art, he did use it in an innovative way by incorporating it into his watercolors and oils. Another possibility is that the innocence and purity associated with childhood found, in Homer's mind, an association with the limpid purity that was so often described as one of watercolor's primary characteristics. It is no small irony, then, that some critics deemed these small works rough, raw, and unfinished—pejoratives provoked by the artist's experiments in *plein-air* work and his attentiveness to the effects of light, both of which called for rapid brushwork resulting in a sketchlike quality.[31]

Critics also found it difficult to accept the dearth of narrative displayed in these watercolors, and in that connection it is interesting to note that if, as it is presumed, the watercolor version of *Waiting for a Bite* was first exhibited as *Why Don't the Suckers Bite?*, the title introduced a stronger narrative element in its suggestion of the boys' conversation.[32] The oil version, however, shares the engraving's title and, what is more, expands on the non-narrative sensibility established in the engraving by augmenting the boys' isolation in a wilderness spot. Homer achieved this effect by eliminating the boy farthest to the right, pushing the figures back in pictorial space, increasing the horizontality of the image, and replacing the verdant backdrop with a barren, deforested landscape. The treeless acres stretching behind the boys automatically suggest the workings of mankind in nature and are contrasted vividly with the natural beauty of the flowers dotting the surface of the lake. Seeds of that opposition exist in the engraving, which shows the boys fully embraced in nature, including forest and lake, whereas the watercolor omits the lake and its botanical features entirely. What becomes apparent is that, as the critics observed in their complaints that his subjects were "rarely anything in themselves,"[33] Homer's concerns went beyond the mere picturing of anecdotal events. In each of the three pictorial variants, his subject was apparently nature, but the grander idea of the changing wilderness assumes priority in the oil, presumably as a result of his having explored the possible permutations of the theme in two "lesser" mediums.

Although iconographic connections between Homer's engravings, watercolors, and oils have long been recognized, the extent to which they reveal the patterns in Homer's approach to narrative content has been underestimated. And, although it is not presumed that Homer's creative process consistently followed the same route, the ideas introduced here seem enough to justify further investigation based on the hypothesis that Homer adjusted his consonant images in conformance with the artistic hierarchies governing the various mediums in which they were executed and according to the thematic gravity that each medium could bear. A general pattern concerning this medium-to-content ratio does emerge: the "lesser" the medium, the "greater" the narrative content. As Homer divested his early oils of overt narrative, they assumed an increasingly modern, indecipherable quality. To decode them, it is necessary to accord the images in each medium equal weight in order to discover the process by which his content evolved.

NOTES

1. The two major sources surveying Homer's freelance career are Philip C. Beam, *Winslow Homer's Magazine Engravings* (New York: Harper & Row, 1979), and David Tatham, *Winslow Homer and the Illustrated Book* (Syracuse, N.Y.: Syracuse University Press, 1992). Each contains a selected bibliography on the subject.

2. Among the most notable publications in which serious effort is placed on linking the iconographies of Homer's engraved, watercolor, and oil images are Nicolai Cikovsky, Jr., "Winslow Homer's *School Time* 'A Picture Thoroughly National,'" in *In Honor of Paul Mellon, Collector and Benefactor,* ed. John Wilmerding (Washington, D.C.: National Gallery of Art, 1986), 47–69; John Wilmerding, "Winslow Homer's *Dad's Coming,*" in *In Honor of Paul Mellon,* 389–401; and Nicolai Cikovsky, Jr., "Winslow Homer's (So-Called) *Morning Bell,*" *American Art Journal* 29, nos. 1 and 2 (1998): 4–17.

3. The commonly cited source verifying that *Sharpshooter* is Homer's first oil is a statement made by his friend Roswell Shurtleff published in "Correspondence. Shurtleff Recalls Homer," *American Art News* 9 (October 29, 1910): 4. It is more than likely that Shurtleff meant that the painting was the first oil that Homer exhibited.

4. See Marc Simpson's entry for the painting in Marc Simpson et al., *Winslow Homer: Paintings of the Civil War,* exh. cat. (San Francisco: The Fine Arts Museums of San Francisco and Bedford Arts, Publishers, 1988), 125–27, in which Simpson provides citations and the scant critical remarks directed to the painting when it was shown in 1864 at the Atheneum Club and at the Artists Reception for the Benefit of the Brooklyn and Long Island Fair, where it was titled *Berdan Sharp-Shooter* (referring to the specialist regiments of sharpshooters led by Colonel Hiram Berdan); and Christopher Kent Wilson, "Marks of Honor and Death, *Sharpshooter* and the Peninsular Campaign of 1862," in Simpson et al., *Winslow Homer: Paintings of the Civil War,* 25–45. In Simpson's volume, Homer's Civil War magazine engravings are integral to the discussion of the paintings.

5. The wood engraving appeared in *Harper's Weekly,* November 15, 1862, 724.

6. Several paragraphs, including quotations from the artist, were devoted to J. A. S. Oertel's *Convalescent Soldiers,* the cover for the issue. A. R. Waud's drawing, *Summit Station on Maryland Heights,* was described under a paragraph headed "The Army of the Potomac" (733). Two drawings by Thomas Nast depicted General George McClellan making his rounds and one of the battles, neither of which required specific commentary because the images so clearly referred to events and personalities of the war. They found context, however, in the column "Domestic Intelligence. Our Army in Virginia" (723), which mentioned McClellan and gave accounts of battles and casualties.

7. Homer expressed these feelings in a letter to George G. Briggs, February 19, 1896 (Archives of American Art, Smithsonian Institution, Washington, D.C.), cited in Nicolai Cikovsky, Jr., and Franklin Kelly, *Winslow Homer,* exh. cat. (Washington, New Haven, London: National Gallery of Art and Yale University Press, 1995), 40.

8. Christopher Kent Wilson also connects the canteen with the target: "In Homer's print, the canteen is not only a mark of the sharpshooter's special status but also a visual metaphor for his skills and deadly tactics. The canteen's dark circle surrounded by a light concentric band suggests a target not unlike the target circle used to test the skills and qualifications of Berdan's marksmen. Ironically, the canteen also alludes in a subtle and cruel way to the enemy whose canteens are literally and figuratively among the sharpshooter's favorite targets" (Simpson et al., *Winslow Homer: Paintings of the Civil War,* 38–39).

9. Apparently Homer had given himself an ultimatum of sorts regarding his entry into the ranks of oil painters. A story handed down in the Homer family asserts that he had vowed to take a full-time position at Harper Brothers if his first oil paintings did not sell. Unbeknownst to Homer, his brother Charles purchased *Sharpshooter* and *In Front of the Guard-House,* 1863 (Canajoharie Library and Art Museum, Canajoharie, New York) anonymously to ensure that his brother would continue painting (Simpson et al., *Winslow Homer: Paintings of the Civil War,* 161). At about this time Homer was treating some of the vignettes in his engravings differently, as if they were isolated designs for paintings done in miniature. This is apparent in *News from the War* (pl. 23) (published in the June 14, 1862 issue of *Harper's Weekly),* in which the motif of the bereaved woman at the top center of the engraving stands apart from those surrounding it because of Homer's care in describing the interior in which she sits and because of the fine detail given each element of this composition-within-a-composition.

10. Although Charles Baudelaire's reputation as a critic and poet may have been known by some North Americans by the 1860s, even by 1871 it seems that his general reputation rested on his role as the translator of Edgar Allan Poe's works into French. See Belgravia, "The French Translator of Poe," *New York Times,* October 29, 1871, 2.

11. Eugene Benson, "The 'Woman Question'," *The Galaxy* 2 (December 15, 1866): 751–56.

12. The exhibition-auction was organized by Henry H. Leeds & Miner, New York, and was held from November 12 to 17, 1866. Homer's and Benson's paintings were part of a larger offering of more important European and American

art. No exhibition catalogue for the section devoted to Homer's and Benson's works has been located. I am grateful to Abigail Booth Gerdts of the Lloyd Goodrich and Edith Havens Goodrich, Whitney Museum of American Art, Record of the Works of Winslow Homer, City University of New York, for providing this information.

13. A small painting attributed to Benson titled *Pensive Moment* (signed "E. Benson" and dated 1865) was offered at Christie's, New York, on December 7, 1984, as lot 70 in *Important American Paintings, Drawings, and Sculpture of the 18th, 19th and 20th Centuries*. The painting is of a contemplative young woman sitting on a porch overlooking a rural landscape. The composition, mood, and pose of the girl bear striking similarities to several works by Homer (especially *Croquet Match*, discussed below), further suggesting that Homer and Benson's relationship was one of mutual influence.

14. David Park Curry, *Winslow Homer: The Croquet Game*, exh. cat. (New Haven, Conn.: Yale University Art Gallery, 1984).

15. "Summer in the Country," *Appletons' Journal of Literature, Science and Art*, July 10, 1869, 465.

16. See Eliza Leslie, *American Girl's Book, or Occupation for Play Hours* (Boston: Munroe and Francis, [1831]), 122–23.

17. For a summary of the etiquette for New Year's calls, see "New Year's Calls," *Harper's Bazar*, January 1, 1870, 3.

18. For a discussion of Homer's *Portrait of Helena de Kay*, see Cikovsky and Kelly, *Winslow Homer*, 122–23. See also Joseph Stanton, "Winslow Homer, Helena de Kay and Richard Watson Gilder: Posing a Rivalry of Forms," *Harvard Library Bulletin*, n.s., 5, no. 2 (Summer 1994): 51–72, for an interesting but unconvincing discussion about Homer's friendship with de Kay.

19. It is often open to question as to the order of word and image.

20. See Cikovsky, "Winslow Homer's *School Time*," in which he discusses what he describes as the "high incidence of signature play in Homer's school paintings" (61–67).

21. In the painting, on the desk at the right, there is a small vase of flowers, which may refer to the schoolmistress's romantic yearnings.

22. For a detailed discussion of *The Old Mill* (also known as *The Morning Bell*), see Cikovsky, "Winslow Homer's (So-Called) *Morning Bell*" (see n. 2).

23. Ibid., 12.

24. See "The Realm of Art. Some Notes on the Academy Spring Exhibition," *New York Evening Telegram*, April 20, 1872, cited in Cikovsky and Kelly, *Winslow Homer*, 92.

25. Cikovsky does not discuss the poem.

26. See page 44 herein.

27. According to Cikovsky and Kelly (*Winslow Homer*, 407), the 1870 painting *The Dinner Horn* was offered at auction at Somerville Gallery, New York, in 1871. Evidently it did not sell, for the work was later given by the artist to Charles Collins of New York.

28. Tatham, *Winslow Homer and the Illustrated Book*, 18.

29. See "Fine Art," *Nation*, February 4, 1875, 84, in which a writer stated: "Aquarelle is a method of art which goes to the adornment of homes, and it partakes largely of the spirit of a decoration or object of furniture; it is more agreeable in proportion as it frankly confesses the quality, leaving to oil the manufacture of great gallery pictures and pieces of didactic authority." Another critic wrote: "Water-color painting seems so especially adapted for happy thoughts, pretty bits of landscape, clever turns of figure that are not quite worth perpetuating in the gravity of oils" ("Watercolors," *New York Times*, January 21, 1877, 7).

30. Helen Cooper, *Winslow Homer Watercolors*, exh. cat. (Washington, D.C., New Haven, London: National Gallery of Art and Yale University Press, 1986), 25.

31. For thorough discussions of Homer's early watercolor aesthetic, see Kathleen Foster, "Makers of the American Watercolor Movement: 1860–1890," Ph.D. dissertation, Yale University, 1982, 56–76; and Cooper, *Winslow Homer Watercolors*, 20–59.

32. For critics' difficulties in assessing Homer's art at this time, see especially Henry James, "On Some Pictures Lately Exhibited," first published in *The Galaxy* in 1875 and reprinted in John L. Sweeney, *The Painter's Eye: Notes and Essays on the Pictorial Arts by Henry James* (Cambridge, Mass.: Harvard University Press, 1956), in which James wrote: "Mr. Homer goes in, as the phrase is, for perfect realism, and cares not a jot for such fantastic hair-splitting as the distinction between beauty and ugliness. . . . He is almost barbarously simple, and, to our eye, he is horribly ugly; but there is nevertheless something one likes about him. What is it? For ourselves, it is not his subjects. We frankly confess that we detest his subjects—his barren plank fences, his glaring, bald, blue skies, his big, dreary, vacant lots of meadows, his freckled, straight-haired Yankee urchins, his flat-breasted maidens, suggestive of a dish of rural doughnuts and pie. . . . He has chosen the least pictorial features of the least pictorial range of scenery and civilization; he has resolutely treated them as if they *were* pictorial" (96–97).

33. "The Watercolor Exhibition," *New York Tribune*, February 19, 1876, 3.

NOTES ON HOMER AND WOOD ENGRAVING

Marilyn S. Kushner

The illustrations that Winslow Homer made for the medium of wood engraving in the first twenty years of his career have been the subject of several exhibitions and many essays. Few, however, have examined these illustrations within the context of their actual production, leaving a number of questions to be more fully explored. For example, exactly what was the state of wood engraving when Homer was active?[1] Who were the professional wood engravers responsible for carving out the images? And how did Homer's images compare with other wood engravings being done at the time? Posing such questions can tell us not only about how these engravings came to be made, but also about their role in Homer's development.

Homer worked in an era when wood-engraved illustrations were in great demand. Moreover, he first gained respect as an accomplished artist at a point in his career when illustrations formed the bulk of his work. His timing was impeccable: he entered the field when it was the medium of choice for reproducing images in the popular press, and he ceased making wood engravings when their influence was being eclipsed by photography. And although he was never a staff artist working exclusively for one company, preferring to remain a freelancer, his success was such that in the eighteen-year period from 1857 to 1875 Homer was able to support himself largely by making these illustrations for the popular press.[2]

✦ ✦ ✦

According to William James Linton, one of the most respected wood engravers of the last half of the nineteenth century, the publication of Adams's Bible in the 1840s by Harper Brothers marked the rise of wood engraving in the United States.[3] Prominent wood engravers, who took great pride in their work, were widely employed by the illustrated weeklies and journals that proliferated beginning in the 1850s. The demand for this kind of reading material, coupled with new printing technologies and the development of a national delivery system by rail, contributed to the robust growth of the medium.[4] By 1850 wood engravings had been printed in *Harper's New Monthly Magazine.* Subsequently, *Frank Leslie's Illustrated Newspaper* first appeared in late 1855, *Harper's Weekly Journal of Civilization* was first published in 1857, and *Ballou's Pictorial Drawing Room Companion* appeared in Boston, also in 1857. Such publications required the services of wood engravers to translate the artists' original images onto printable surfaces. In the 1850s, the principal subjects were landscapes and portraits, and relatively few illustrations had political or social content. However, amid the volatile politics of the years just before the Civil War, the public soon began to clamor for views of current events.

The milieu of the wood engravers in New York was quite small, and virtually all of them knew each other. "Most of the Engravers were established in a narrow section," wrote Elbridge Kingsley (1842–1900), a wood engraver active from the 1860s through the 1890s.[5] He continued, "Frank Leslie's Weekly, corner of Elm & Pearl Streets and Harper's Weekly, corner of Cliff and Pearl Streets, employed a great number on the coarser picture work. Smaller firms doing a variety of work were crowded into the upper lofts on the east of Broadway, between John Street south and Spruce Street on the north." One very popular building for the engravers was 48 Beekman Street. Here, Kingsley worked with Edward Sears, who employed a large number of wood engravers on various projects.[6] According to Kingsley, individual engravers tended to specialize in particular kinds of imagery. Some were best at depicting machinery, for example, while others worked on landscape; some were better at carving fine lines, while certain others worked on the "bolder line needed in a work like the Picturesque America."[7]

The offices Kingsley describes must have been similar to those that Homer frequented when he was in New York during these years:

> On the first floor were the artists, and perhaps the apprentices who helped in general ways, from cutting away wood and proving to the running of errands. The engravers on the upper floor were arranged according to the number of windows and the adaptability of the light. Generally three men to a window seated at a three cornered desk, all facing the light as much as possible. A north light was preferred to any other. Each man's belongings consisted of his set of tools, a sandbag to rest his block upon, and an eyeglass in a convenient frame to swing at any angle and focus upon his work. For night work an ordinary fish globe filled with water served to focus the light from a lamp on the block with sufficient intensity. This round spot of intense light was as good as daylight. An oil stone for sharpening the tools, and perhaps a paper shade for the eyes, constituted the outfit of the engraver. If he was to do work at home, he rolled up his [tools] in a paper, put them in his pocket, and with his block under his arm, arranged himself in the same way at his own center table. . . . The routine of the engraver consisted in keeping his block in good shape while in his hands. Generally he kept the surface covered excepting the spot being cut

at the moment. This was done by waxing the sides and covering over with a thin brown paper, and pulling it tight over the edges, then making a hole to work through with the edge of the graver. If the engraver had more than one block on hand at once, he always kept the idle block standing on its edge; to avoid a chance of warping, or of something hitting the surface.[8]

While the engravers usually worked together at the publishers' offices, the artists often worked in their own studios. An artist would be given a block that had been covered with a white substance resembling watercolor. The artist drew the image on this surface. The block was then returned to the publisher and assigned to the appropriate wood engraver. If a number of blocks had been bolted together for the artist to create a larger image, often they would be separated by the publishers and given to different wood engravers to carve. This was more efficient when facing a deadline, as was often the case at the illustrated weeklies. "The blocks were made up of parts bolted together," Kingsley noted. "Mr Patterson, the foreman, would cut across the joints, and then give out the pieces to each man, whose business it was to match it and sit up till it was finished. This was a racing match rather than a growth in Art."[9] We do not know of any instance in which Homer engraved his own block.[10] This division of labor was the standard practice, since the skills needed to engrave the block were quite different from those necessary to draw the original image.

This was still the era when a good wood engraver would "interpret" the image that he was carving, rather than make a literal translation of the composition into wood. That is, the wood engraver's duty was to render the spirit of the artist's intent. Therefore, if the artist indicated clouds, they would be carved out not necessarily by exactly following all the marks he had made, but rather by cutting the types of line that the wood engravers traditionally used to *symbolize* clouds. Similarly, there were established methods of depicting other elements of landscape, figures, and so on. This explains Kingsley's remark that some engravers were better at landscape and others at machinery: distinct components of an image called for different carving treatments. The strength of Winslow Homer's designs, and the reason many wood engravers admired his work, was precisely that his drawings were tailored to the engravers' needs, making his designs very easy to follow and interpret.

In the 1870s and 1880s, wood engravers' methods changed, creating great controversy within this tightly knit community. The new Impressionist style, with its large areas of tonality and less concretely defined figures and objects, was not easy to translate into the engraving medium using traditional linear methods. As a result, a so-called New School of wood engravers began to translate in a literal way virtually *every* mark the artist had made in his image.

In this new method, there was no longer room for interpretation by the wood engraver.[11] Moreover, the use of photography in reproduction threatened the art of the wood engravers unless they, too, were willing to copy the original drawings faithfully.

When Homer began making his images for the illustrated weeklies, the field was still very traditional, and the linear style of illustration, as taught to him in Boston by Charles Damoreau, was well suited to the older school of wood engraving. However, by the time he stopped working for the illustrated press, the controversy was raging, and Homer probably benefited from it: the wood engravers of the New School were better able to reproduce his later, more painterly watercolor images.

◆　◆　◆

Homer began making wood engravings in Boston, after leaving his apprenticeship at John H. Bufford's lithography workshop in 1857. By the summer of 1857, he had met Charles Damoreau, who had begun carving Homer's images for *Ballou's Pictorial*. Damoreau was a French wood engraver active in Boston from 1856 to 1860.[12] Since Homer had just spent three years in a lithography shop, his images were more in keeping with the lithographic process—that is, they were more tonal than linear. It was Damoreau who taught Homer how to draw for the wood engravers, a skill that Homer picked up quickly and refined throughout his illustrational career. In these early works, such as *Corner of Winter, Washington and Summer Streets, Boston* (pl. 1), from *Ballou's Pictorial*,

Fig. 1. Winslow Homer. *Class Day, at Harvard University, Cambridge Mass.*, from *Ballou's Pictorial Drawing Room Companion*, July 3, 1858, p. 2. Wood engraving, 5½ x 9⅜ inches (14 x 23.8 cm). Alexander Library, Rutgers University, New Brunswick, New Jersey. Photograph by Chris Bartels

CLASS DAY, AT HARVARD UNIVERSITY, CAMBRIDGE, MASS.

June 13, 1857, an emphasis on heavy linearity overcompensates for the fact that the tonal tint of the lithograph cannot be achieved so readily in a wood engraving. Certainly Damoreau, the engraver of this image, knew how to achieve degrees of light and dark, but these would have had to be indicated in Homer's drawing. Quite likely, the original drawing (which, obviously, no longer exists, having been carved away in the process of making the wood engraving) was an attempt by the inexperienced Homer to draw in the linear

THE "HARVARD," WINNER OF THE RACE FOR SIX-OARED BOATS, ON THE CHARLES RIVER, BOSTON, JUNE 19, 1858.

Fig. 2. Alfred Waud. *The "Harvard," Winner of the Race for Six-Oared Boats, on the Charles River, Boston, June 19, 1858,* from *Harper's Weekly,* July 3, 1858, p. 429. Wood engraving, 6 x 9 ½ inches (15.2 x 24.1 cm). Art Reference Library, Brooklyn Museum of Art

manner throughout the composition. The shading, here stiff and lacking graduated tones, would become far more delicate in Homer's later wood-engraved images.

We know the identities of a few other wood engravers who worked on Homer's early images in Boston, since many of the illustrations that Homer did for *Ballou's Pictorial* were signed by the carver (apparently the journal's policy).[13] Besides Damoreau, the name that appears most often is William Pierce (active 1851–70), followed by George Hayes (died 1873), Edmund N. Tarbell (active in Boston 1857–60), and Frederick E. Fox (active in Boston 1856–60).[14] Pierce was a wood engraver who worked in Boston from 1851 until about 1870. For a few short years in the 1850s, he seems to have been with the firm of Worcester & Pierce, but he apparently left the company and began to do wood engravings for other publishers. Hayes was another wood engraver active in Boston in the 1850s, and a great deal of his work was done for *Ballou's Pictorial.* Tarbell, a New Yorker who spent just a few years in

Boston between 1857 and 1860, boarded in the home of Hammatt Billings (1816–1874) in 1860. Coincidentally, Billings also drew for *Ballou's Pictorial* in the late 1850s, when Homer was working there. The two worked together again in New York in the 1860s, illustrating William Barnes's 1869 edition of *Rural Poems.*[15]

We know that while in Boston, Homer shared studio space with the brothers William (1830–1878) and Alfred Waud (1828–1891), two English artist-illustrators who had probably come to the United States about 1858.[16] Since Homer was in New York by 1859, they must have been with him shortly after their arrival, and quite possibly communicated to him the British appreciation of wood engraving. All three men were employed as artists by *Harper's Weekly* during the Civil War.

Even in the 1850s, Homer's work was more specific than that of these fellow illustrators, perhaps because he was more interested in representing typical

THE BATHE AT NEWPORT.

Fig. 3. Winslow Homer. *The Bathe at Newport,* from *Harper's Weekly,* September 4, 1858, p. 568. Wood engraving, 9 ¼ x 13 ¼ inches (23.5 x 34.9 cm). 1998.105.18, Gift of Harvey Isbitts, Brooklyn Museum of Art

contemporary American life than in depicting general geographical views. In his busy images he gave the flavor and detail of Boston as no other artist had previously—even the shop signs were readable and familiar to those Bostonians who knew the area depicted. When one compares Homer's early scenes (fig. 1) stylistically with an image such as Alfred Waud's *The "Harvard," Winner of the Race for Six-Oared Boats, on the Charles River, Boston, June*

THE ATLANTIC TELEGRAPH EXPEDITION—THE "NIAGARA" AND THE "AGAMEMNON" IN THE GALE.—[See First Page.]

Fig. 4. Anonymous. *The Atlantic Telegraph Expedition—The "Niagara" and the "Agamemnon" in the Gale*, from *Harper's Weekly*, August 14, 1858, p. 521. Wood engraving, 9 ¹³⁄₁₆ x 13 inches (25.1 x 33 cm). Art Reference Library, Brooklyn Museum of Art

19, 1858 (fig. 2), Homer's figures look energetic and strong, as opposed to the very linear and rigid ones by Waud. Still, Homer's early figures are diminutive in comparison to the large, confident ones that dominated his later compositions.[17]

Another comparison—between Homer's *The Bathe at Newport* (fig. 3) and a contemporaneous illustration by an unknown artist, *The Atlantic Telegraph Expedition—The "Niagara" and the "Agamemnon" in the Gale* (fig. 4)—is indicative of the young Boston artist's skill already at this early stage in his career. Whereas Homer's depiction of the movement of water, even within the linear medium of wood engraving, has an energized life, the water in the anonymous ship scene remains stilted. A similar comparison can be made with the cover illustration for *Harper's Weekly* of September 11, 1858, *The Atlantic Cable Celebration—The Niagaras in Broadway* (fig. 5), also by an unknown artist. One would expect to see movement and animation in such a celebration. Instead, the figures are frozen in space. Yet Homer at this early date was able to depict playful action in his wood engravings, as evidenced by the movement of his figures as they romp in the water at the Newport beach. When considered alongside contemporaneous images, Homer's work often shows an awkward grace that developed, very shortly, into the elegance of line for which the artist is known.

By October 1859 Homer was living in New York. He rented a room in a boardinghouse on East Sixteenth Street for two years, then moved to the New York University Building on Washington Square, staying there for more than ten years. His neighbors in the Washington Square building included the genre painters Eastman Johnson (1824–1906) and William Hennessey (1839–1917). Homer knew Hennessey, who was also an active illustrator.

Hennessey was born in Ireland and came to the United States with his family when he was ten years old. His art was first shown at the National Academy of Design in 1857. He worked for a wood engraver in the late 1850s and was a prolific book illustrator throughout the 1860s, remaining in New York until his departure for London in 1870. He drew for *Every Saturday,* as did Homer, and some of his images, like some of Homer's, were engraved by William J. Linton, who was one of the leading wood engravers of the time. Such ties, as well as the fact that their studios were opposite each other in the Washington Square building, probably drew the two artists to each other. A comparison of their work shows that, while both were considered fine artists, Homer's illustrations have a delicate finesse not present in the Irish artist's work. In 1870 Hennessey drew the images for *Edwin Booth in Twelve Dramatic Characters.*[18] His image of Booth as Hamlet (fig. 6) is strong, and the figure looms as a major force in the composition. The design was engraved by Linton and displays the technical virtuosity for which the engraver was renowned, especially in the architectural detail on the right of the composition. However, when one compares this figure with Homer's *The Dinner Horn* (pl. 48), which appeared in *Harper's Weekly* on June 11, 1870, the mastery of Homer's design becomes quite clear. Homer's image of the young woman contains nuances of delicate line and definition that sharply contrast with the brutal strength of Hennessey's Hamlet. The best result that Linton could produce for

Fig. 5. Anonymous. *The Atlantic Cable Celebration—The Niagaras in Broadway,* from *Harper's Weekly,* September 11, 1858, p. 577. Wood engraving, 10⅜ x 9⅛ inches (27 x 23.2 cm). Art Reference Library, Brooklyn Museum of Art

Hennessey, one of the most respected illustrators of the time, was not as fine as Homer's work.

Homer had done illustrations for *Harper's Weekly* before he arrived in New York, having produced more than twenty-five images for the journal while he was still in Boston, between 1857 and the fall of 1859. As far as we know, his illustrations appeared exclusively in *Harper's Weekly* from early 1860 until 1865, at which time he began illustrating for *Frank Leslie's Chimney Corner* as well (one illustration in June 1865 and another in December of that year). Most of the illustrative work that Homer did during the Civil War for *Harper's Weekly* was associated with the war effort. However, following the cessation of hostilities, Homer cast his eye elsewhere, as did the rest of the country.[19] He began to make images about leisure pursuits, women, and children at the same time that he began working for other publications.

By the end of 1865, when Homer had broken away from his reliance on *Harper's Weekly*, his images began appearing in a number of publications, including *Frank Leslie's Illustrated Newspaper, Our Young Folks, The Riverside Magazine for Young People,* and *Harper's Bazar.* Quite certainly, by the mid-1860s Homer's growing reputation as an important painter as well as an illustrator drew the atten-

Fig. 6. William Hennessey. *Hamlet,* from *Edwin Booth in Twelve Dramatic Characters,* by William Winter (Boston: James R. Osgood & Company, 1872), n.p. Wood engraving, 11 x 8 inches (27.9 x 20.3 cm). Benjamin Rosenthal Library, Queens College, New York

tion of the additional publications that now sought his work. Not only was Homer able to obtain remuneration from other publishing concerns, but as a more established artist, he commanded the services of the most accomplished wood engravers. Homer's working method was described by James Edward Kelly, a younger artist then learning the trade. From the account, one can see that the young Winslow Homer was already greeted with respect at the publishing establishment:

> *Mr. Parsons [Charles Parsons, head of the art department at* Harper's Weekly*], greeted him as Mr. Homer. They sat down*

while Mr. Parsons looked over the drawing which he had brought, and made some suggestions; then Homer went to Davis's desk and started to work on the block. Reinhart and Abbey left their places and stood by watching him work. Occasionally he would stop and chat with them.... Mr. Parsons was quite critical, and would make suggestions which Homer took in good part, and at once made the corrections.[20]

Most *Harper's Weekly* wood engravers did not sign the images on which they worked until 1873.[21] From Homer's illustrations that began to appear in other journals, which did allow the wood engravers to sign their work, we can again garner information on the men who carved the compositions and prepared them for publication.

John Karst and John Parker Davis were among those who engraved Homer's images for *Frank Leslie's Chimney Corner* in 1865 and among the first wood-engraver signatures to be seen on a Homer image since his work in Boston. Karst (1836–1911) was born in Germany and brought to the United States as an infant. His first known wood engraving is dated 1855. Davis (1832–1910), who learned the art of wood engraving in Philadelphia, worked for both *Scribner's Monthly* and *Harper's Weekly,* and served as superintendent of the engraving department of *Frank Leslie's Weekly.* By the early 1880s, his work was so well known (he would eventually replace William Linton as the teacher of engraving at the Cooper Union) that he was reproducing Mary Cassatt's images in the popular presses. And Davis's wood engraving was so respected by the artists with whom he worked that Elbridge Kingsley, one of Davis's colleagues, wrote, "I think Davis was the only one of this group [of the New School of engravers] who had the enthusiasm to take hold and grow with the younger men of the future."[22] Eventually, he became the founder and secretary to the Society of American Wood Engravers.

While Davis began his career as a promoter of the traditional view of wood engraving, in the 1870s he became an ardent supporter of the New School. He stated: "The more the original artist's work appears in the engraving, unobscured by the personality of the engraver—the more brush marks there are and the fewer tool marks—the better is the effect produced. This is the purpose of the conscientious engraver."[23]

Aside from *Frank Leslie's Chimney Corner,* Davis and Karst also engraved Homer's images that appeared in periodicals such as *Appletons' Journal of Literature, Science and Art, Every Saturday,* and *Our Young Folks.* Other wood engravers who worked on Homer illustrations included Andrew Varick Stout Anthony, G. A. Avery, John Filmer, W. H. Kingdon, W. H. Lagarde, James L. Langridge, William J. Linton, W. H. Morse, William H. Redding, and H. Wolf. Of these men, the best known was Linton.

Linton (1812–1897), who engraved Hennessey's images (such as Booth's Hamlet, fig. 6) and illustrations for books by Henry Wadsworth Longfellow and John Greenleaf Whittier, was a British wood engraver who came to the United States in 1866. His reputation had been established in London, where he had engraved for notable artists, including Dante Gabriel Rossetti. Because of his stature as a wood engraver in England, when Linton arrived in New York he immediately became one of the "foremost engraver[s] of the time."[24] He taught wood engraving at the Cooper Union, and in 1880 he wrote *The History of Wood-Engraving in America.* Throughout his career, Linton championed the traditional view of wood engraving, as opposed to the New School.

Andrew Varick Stout Anthony (1835–1906), a disciple of Linton's, studied drawing and engraving under T. W. Strong. He spent part of the 1860s in California and New York, and eventually settled in Boston in the 1870s. In 1881 it was written of Anthony that "we have no engraver who is more distinctly native to our soil, or who possesses more capacity in treating every variety of subject."[25] Anthony did not work on Homer's illustrations for the weeklies, but rather engraved Homer's images for Longfellow's "Excelsior," published in 1878 in *Christmastide,* a gift book. He was known for the illustrated books that he engraved. Other volumes that he worked on included *Gems from Tennyson* (1866), *The Vision of Sir Launfal* (1867), by James Russell, and *Ballads of New England* (1870), by Whittier. He also worked with Linton on Longfellow's *Building of the Ship* (1870). In Boston, Anthony did a large amount of book work for Fields, Osgood & Company, the firm that also published the journal *Every Saturday,* which first began illustrating images in the late 1860s. *Every Saturday* was intended to compete with *Harper's Weekly,* and Homer immediately began working for the new journal. It was probably through his work with this publishing firm that Homer came into contact with Anthony.

Fig. 7. Alfred Waud. *Pictures of the South: Magnolia Grove, on the Shell Road at Mobile, Alabama,* from *Harper's Weekly,* September 8, 1866, p. 561 (cover). Wood engraving, 11 x 9¾ inches (27.9 x 24.8 cm). Art Reference Library, Brooklyn Museum of Art

Homer's achievement in wood engraving becomes clear when we compare his post–Civil War illustrations with those of two of the most prolific illustrators of the period: Alfred Waud and Thomas Nast.

Waud's *Magnolia Grove, on the Shell Road at Mobile, Alabama* (fig. 7), from his *Pictures of the South,* appeared as a cover image in *Harper's Weekly* on September 8, 1866.[26] In contrast to the elegance of Homer's figures in *Our National Winter Exercise—Skating* (pl. 57), which appeared in *Frank Leslie's Illustrated Newspaper* on January 13, 1866, Waud's figures are rugged and lack the cultivated grace of Homer's skaters. Waud's individuals have no facial expression or emotion, while Homer's do express sentiments—embar-

"THE PIRATES," UNDER FALSE COLORS.—CAN THEY CAPTURE THE SHIP OF STATE?

Fig. 8. Thomas Nast. *The Pirates, under False Colors.—Can They Capture the Ship of State?*, from *Harper's Weekly,* November 9, 1872, p. 872. Wood engraving, 13¾ x 20¾ inches (34.9 x 52.7 cm). Art Reference Library, Brooklyn Museum of Art

rassment, in the case of the woman who has taken a tumble on the right, and demure reticence, in the case of the woman who is accompanied by a man at the rear. The delicacy of Homer's lines enlivens the scene. The folds of the women's dresses as defined by the wavy lines that pulsate with motion (especially in the central figure) belie any claim that a linear style had to be stiff and static.

Nast's images are bold and roughly drawn. His style was brusque, as were his biting commentaries on politics. Though Homer's images were not as politically motivated, comparing his *Homeward Bound* (pl. 43), from *Harper's Weekly,* December 21, 1867, with Nast's *The Pirates, under False Colors.—Can They Capture the Ship of State?* (fig. 8) is instructive. Both images depict scenes on a ship's deck packed with figures. Homer's figures are genteel and delicate, appropriate to his subject of sophisticated people returning to America after European holidays. Nast's characters, however, are politicians mainly concerned with preserving their power. The harshly drawn lines seen here are typical of his style: they are the marks of an illustrator whose goal is a strongly opinionated "message" rather than an elegant composition. Homer's illustration is the work of an artist, a master of the medium, whose images speak of technical excellence as well as aesthetic beauty.

◆   ◆   ◆

Winslow Homer worked as an illustrator during the era when reproduction of hand-drawn images, as opposed to photographic ones, was the popular mode of illustration. It was also an age when the general populace called for pictorial accounts of important current events and when it began to rely on visual narratives, whether as addenda to verbal storytelling or as independent entities that could recount a tale or event without the written word. The weeklies filled these burgeoning needs, with the help of the illustrators and wood engravers. Homer, supporting himself as a young artist in these years, built up a store of experience that became the foundation for the rest of his career. At the same time, he established a reputation as one of the finest of all illustrators.

1. The best scholarly discussion of these issues is in David Tatham, *Winslow Homer and the Illustrated Book* (Syracuse, N.Y.: Syracuse University Press, 1992), 1–20.

2. Winslow Homer so intensely disliked his three years of apprenticeship at John H. Bufford's lithography shop in Boston (1854–57) that on the day he turned twenty-one, he quit and vowed never to work for anyone else again. In the future, he always freelanced to earn his living.

3. W. J. Linton, *The History of Wood-Engraving in America* (Boston: Estes & Lauriat, 1881), 22.

4. Tatham, *Winslow Homer and the Illustrated Book*, 2. Among the technological developments was the electrotype, which began to be widely used in printing the new publications. A wax mold was made of the wood-engraved image, and a thin metal plate was taken from that mold. This final plate was so thin and pliable that it could be wrapped around the cylinders of printing presses. Not only was this process faster than anything used previously, but more than one metal plate could be made from a mold, allowing more presses to be deployed and more copies of a publication to be produced in a shorter amount of time.

5. Elbridge Kingsley, "Life and Works of Elbridge Kingsley Painter-Engraver Consisting of Paintings in Oil and Water Colors, Photographs from Paintings reproduced in Engraving, Japan proofs & Plain Prints Experiments with Process Plate," n.d. Elbridge Kingsley Papers, Archives of American Art, Smithsonian Institution, Washington, D.C., reel 119, frame 474.

6. Coincidentally, 48 Beekman Street was where Samuel Putnam Avery, a collector who was also a wood engraver, had his offices from 1851 until 1862. The building was called the Brother Jonathan building, as Benjamin Day published his *Brother Jonathan* weeklies there. See Ruth Sieben-Morgen, "Samuel Putnam Avery (1822–1904), Engraver on Wood: A Bio-Bibliographical Study" (master's thesis, Columbia University, 1940; revised, with additions, 1942), 30.

7. Kingsley, "Life and Works of Elbridge Kingsley Painter-Engraver," reel 119, frame 483. Published between 1872 and 1874, the series *Picturesque America* contained essays and wood-engraved images about different parts of the United States.

8. Ibid., frames 484–85.

9. Ibid., frame 480.

10. We also do not know of the existence of any Homer woodblocks, since the wood was usually shaved down and reused.

11. For further information on this passionate controversy, which consumed the wood-engraving community, see Linton, *The History of Wood-Engraving in America*, passim; and "A Symposium of Wood-Engravers," *Harper's New Monthly Magazine*, February 1880, 442–53. Linton's book represented the traditional school of wood engraving, whereas the entire controversy was heatedly discussed in the symposium in the 1880 publication. For an excellent contemporaneous discussion of the controversy, see also Kingsley, "Life and Works of Elbridge Kingsley Painter-Engraver," reel 119, frames 439–566. For a more recent discussion, see Estelle Jussim, *Visual Communication and the Graphic Arts* (New York: R. R. Bowker Company, 1974), 157–66.

12. Charles Damoreau was considered to be a "48er," an artisan who fled the European revolutions of 1848 and came to America. Schooled in Europe, the 48ers had received far better training in wood engraving than had their American counterparts, who had few opportunities to be taught the trade in a formal setting. For a discussion of the 48ers, see Tatham, *Winslow Homer and the Illustrated Book*, 10–11.

13. This was not the case at *Harper's Weekly*, in New York, where Homer's work was not signed by a wood engraver until 1873, although after 1865 some of Homer's images in other journals in New York were signed by the engraver.

14. William Pierce's name has also been spelled Peirce.

15. Hammatt Billings illustrated the first edition of Harriet Beecher Stowe's *Uncle Tom's Cabin* (1852). Billings was a Boston architect, designer, and illustrator whose work, some feel, influenced Homer's. However, it was not long before the young Homer outpaced his senior (Billings was eighteen years older): while Homer received only two dollars for a drawing in 1857, as opposed to Billings's nine dollars per drawing in 1858, by 1865 Homer was earning twenty-five to thirty dollars for the large images that appeared in *Harper's Weekly*. For a discussion of Billings and of the earnings of both artists, see Tatham, *Winslow Homer and the Illustrated Book*, 14.

16. Others working in Boston at the time included Robert David Wilkie and W. L. Champney. See Tatham, *Winslow Homer and the Illustrated Book*, 11–18; and David Tatham, "Winslow Homer as an Illustrator," in Katherine S. Howe, *Winslow Homer Graphics* (Houston: The Museum of Fine Arts, 1977), 8.

17. See, for example, *The Dinner Horn* (pl. 48), from *Harper's Weekly*, June 11, 1870. Even those late compositions that do not contain a single looming figure but rather a grouping of figures—as in *Raid on a Sand-Swallow Colony—"How Many Eggs?"* (pl. 38), from *Harper's Weekly*, June 13, 1874—exhibit an assured solidity in which the figures define the space of the image.

18. William Winter, *Edwin Booth in Twelve Dramatic*

Characters (Boston: James R. Osgood & Company, 1872). The portraits were by William Hennessey and were engraved by W. J. Linton.

19. After 1865, not only issues related to Reconstruction but also questions about the status of women and children in society, as well as the development of leisure time, became subjects of general interest.

20. James Edward Kelly, James Edward Kelly Papers, Archives of American Art, Smithsonian Institution, Washington, D.C., reel 1876.

21. There were a few exceptions, and in rare instances wood engravers did sign the images. Examples include *Lieutenant General Grant and Staff,* July 15, 1865, signed "Jewett" on the lower left; and *Overland Mail-Coach Crossing the Rocky Mountains—Scene in Guy's Gulch,* February 8, 1868, signed "C.P." on the lower right. Quite possibly, "C.P." was Charles Parsons, head of the art department at *Harper's Weekly.*

22. Kingsley, "Life and Works of Elbridge Kingsley Painter-Engraver," reel 119, frame 480.

23. "A Symposium of Wood-Engravers," 447.

24. Kingsley, "Life and Works of Elbridge Kingsley Painter-Engraver," reel 119, frame 479.

25. S. G. W. Benjamin, "A.V. S. Anthony," chapter 11 of *Our American Artists,* second series (Boston: D. Lothrop & Co., 1881), 61. Facsimile reprint, edited and with an introduction by H. Barbara Weinberg (New York: Garland Publishing, 1977).

26. Declared the most important illustrator-correspondent of the war by *Harper's,* Waud had been sent to the South after the cessation of hostilities to document Reconstruction.

PLATES

All works are in the collection of the Brooklyn Museum of Art, gifts of Harvey Isbitts. Dimensions of wood engravings refer to image size, height preceding width. Engravers are identified when known. The commentaries accompanying the plates are by Marilyn S. Kushner, Barbara Dayer Gallati, and Linda S. Ferber.

EARLY WORK

Homer's apprenticeship at the age of eighteen in 1854 to John H. Bufford in Boston introduced him to lithography and the discipline of drawing designs for commercial illustration. Much of his early work involved copying or reworking a wide repertoire of sentimental images and decorative conventions used in the advertisements and sheet-music title pages that formed a large portion of Bufford's business. Although he quickly became an accomplished copyist, reworking and adapting existing designs, Homer summarized his distaste for the apprenticeship in a later comment: "From the time I took my nose off that lithographic stone, I have had no master, and never shall have any." [1]

After his training ended in 1857, Homer began a long career as a freelance illustrator. His work for *Ballou's Pictorial Drawing Room Companion,* an illustrated weekly published in Boston, demonstrates how rapidly he mastered designing images for wood-engraved illustration. The importance of skilled engravers to realize these designs is signified by the double billing in these early works; later in his New York career, he collaborated with some of the finest wood engravers of the period. Homer's emergence as an independent talent is charted by the evolution of his signature in the *Ballou's* series from "W. H." to "Homer" to mention in texts as "Our artist, Mr. Homer." These lively urban views and accompanying texts appealed to the reader's pride in Boston's mercantile wealth, as well as its public works and nightlife; the latter were celebrated as among the "modern innovations" that placed the metropolis in the company of other great cities like New York and Paris.

—LSF

---

1. David Tatham, "Some Apprentice Lithographs of Winslow Homer—Ten Pictorial Title Pages for Sheet Music," *Old Time New England* (April–June 1969): 94 and passim.

CORNER OF WINTER, WASHINGTON AND SUMMER STREETS, BOSTON.

1. *Corner of Winter, Washington and Summer Streets, Boston,* from *Ballou's Pictorial Drawing Room Companion,* June 13, 1857, cover

Wood engraving, 7 x 9¾ inches (17.9 x 24.8 cm). Engraved by Charles F. Damoreau. 1998.105.2, Gift of Harvey Isbitts

The local view upon this page, drawn expressly for us by Mr. Winslow Homer, a promising young artist of this city, is exceedingly faithful in architectural detail and spirited in character, and represents one of the busiest and most brilliant spots in all Boston.... The figures introduced in our sketch, give a good idea of the character and bustle of this part of the city in the busiest part of the day. Here we have a carriage dashing up at rather an illegal rate of speed which might endanger the lady at the crossing, but for the gentlemanly policeman who is stationed here to ensure the safety of pedestrians ... and who steps forward to lend his assistance and interpose his potential authority.... Promenaders of both sexes, and pedestrians of all ages, complete the lively picture. At this point, Washington Street presents many of the characteristics of Broadway, New York. In the human tide that pours through it there is nearly the same diversity of feature and origin, and the amount of passing is perhaps larger in proportion to the size of the city, crowding the sidewalks full.

(From the text published with the engraving, cover)

VIEW IN SOUTH MARKET STREET, BOSTON.

2. *View in South Market Street, Boston,* from *Ballou's Pictorial Drawing Room Companion,* October 3, 1857, cover

Wood engraving, 6½ x 9½ inches (16.7 x 24.2 cm). Engraved by Charles F. Damoreau. 1998.105.8, Gift of Harvey Isbitts

The busy scene depicted on this page by our artist, Mr. Homer, is a faithful representation, sketched for us from the life, of a highly characteristic Boston scene. Quincy Market is dear to the heart.... Our sketch was made outside the market-house in South Market Street.... For its entire length, there are rows of market carts standing in tiers.... As soon as it is light, customers appear— provision dealers, boarding-house people, heads of poor families.... The maw of a great city like Boston is a very ravenous one, and the sight of the viands and vegetables requisite for a day's supply, combined in one mass, is absolutely startling.

(From the text published with the engraving, cover)

BOSTON EVENING STREET SCENE, AT THE CORNER OF COURT AND BRATTLE STREETS.

3. *Boston Evening Street Scene, at the Corner of Court and Brattle Streets,*
from *Ballou's Pictorial Drawing Room Companion,* November 7, 1857, cover

Wood engraving, 6½ x 9½ inches (16.7 x 24.2 cm). 1998.105.12. Gift of Harvey Isbitts

Mr. Homer has here drawn for us a spirited and graphic picture sketched at the corner of Brattle and Court Streets, in the early part of a fine evening.... There is Holton's shoe-store at the corner, and next to it, down Brattle Street, the famous oyster-house, where we have eaten many a supper in days gone by. Across the way, in Tremont Row, we see Cutting & Turner's great daguerreotype establishment.... Here are a brace of omnibuses.... On the sidewalk of Brattle Street is one of those pulling machines, which measure a man's strength to a fraction. A group is collected round one of Alvan Clark's fine telescopes, in charge of a peripatetic astronomer, gazing at [the] moon.... Ladies and gentlemen promenading, news-boys vending their printed wares, complete the busy picture.... [T]he streets of Boston furnish a good deal of incident and bustle of an evening, and many an interesting adventure follows the shadows of twilight, to give life and vivacity to nocturnal out-of-door existence.

(From the text published with the engraving, cover)

Literary Illustration

Homer's career as a freelance illustrator may be divided roughly between his work for mass-circulation periodicals that documented events or trends of a topical nature and his work that was commissioned to illustrate specific passages in prose or poetry. He pursued both types of illustration from the beginning, with his first notable engravings for works of fiction appearing in 1857 in *The Careless Girl Reformed, and Other Stories,* a collection of moralizing tales for children.[1] The need for illustrators was at its peak in the United States during the time of Homer's activity in the field. This demand was mainly a result of the huge growth in the American publishing industry in general and of the establishment in these years, in particular, of a number of illustrated literary monthlies such as *Scribner's* and *The Galaxy.*

Homer was engaged to illustrate a variety of poems, short stories, and novels of both "high" and "low" literary merit, yet the caliber of the writing seems to have had little or no correlation with the quality of the drawings that he created. It seems that Homer was at his best when interpreting popular literature focusing on contemporary subjects rather than when he was called upon to depict symbolic or elevated themes from the pens of such esteemed literary figures as Henry Wadsworth Longfellow.[2] This discrepancy probably had much to do with his own interests as an artist whose oil paintings were devoted to the here and now of American life.

Strong relationships are often found between some of Homer's illustrations and his more famous and now highly revered oils and watercolors. Such links between his commercial work and his paintings serve as reminders that, although illustration provided a comfortable income for Homer, his goals were fixed on success in the "higher" arts. When possible, he seems to have used his illustration assignments to explore and develop a style related to his independent pursuits as a painter.   —BDG

---

1. For a checklist of Homer's illustrations of prose and poetry for publication in books and periodicals, see David Tatham, *Winslow Homer and the Illustrated Book* (Syracuse, N.Y.: Syracuse University Press, 1992), 289–305.
2. In 1877 Homer provided four drawings for engravings illustrating Longfellow's "Excelsior" for compilation in *Christmastide* (Boston: James R. Osgood & Co., 1878).

OUR WATERING-PLACES—THE EMPTY SLEEVE AT NEWPORT.—[See Page 534.]

4. *Our Watering Places—The Empty Sleeve at Newport,* from *Harper's Weekly,* August 26, 1865, p. 532

Wood engraving, 9 ¼ x 13 ¾ inches (23.5 x 35.1 cm). 1998.105.91, Gift of Harvey Isbitts

This illustration accompanied a story in *Harper's Weekly,* "The Empty Sleeve at Newport; or, Why Edna Ackland Learned to Drive." Captain Harry Ash, having lost an arm, returns from the war to discover that his love, Edna Ackland, has learned to drive a horse and buggy in his absence. The returning men confronted women who had adjusted to changed circumstances and sometimes took a stronger role in the relationship. Harry Ash is described as having "young . . . old-fashioned prejudices. He liked womanly women. . . . [H]e had loved [her] because she seemed so womanly and gentle—a dainty thing to be watched over and guarded from harm—driving with the daring eyes of fops and roués turned upon her, eager for her praise and admiration, forgetful of him and his opinion. . . . He had hoped to find her watching for him—to meet her somewhere quite alone." Captain Ash and Edna Ackland resolve their misunderstandings as she explains to him, "I must be left and right hand [for you] also, should it be God's pleasure. . . . [A]nd I learned, as I have learned many things, for love of you." The dominance of the nineteenth-century male prevails in the end: "Yet, for all that, his eye is on the road and his voice guides her; so that, in reality, she is only his left hand, and he, the husband, drives" (534).

—MSK

GREEN APPLES.

5. *Green Apples,* from *Our Young Folks,* June 1868, frontispiece

Wood engraving, 6 x 3¾ inches (15.4 x 9.6 cm). 1998.105.116, Gift of Harvey Isbitts

Pull down the bough, Bob! Isn't this fun?
Now give it a shake, and—there goes one!
Now, put your thumb up to the other, and see
If it isn't as mellow as mellow can be!
    I know by the stripe
    It must be ripe!
That's one apiece for you and me.

. . . .

"For the youth there's love, just streaked with
   red,
And great joys hanging just over his head;
Happiness, honor, and great estate,
For those who patiently work and wait;—
    Blessings," said he [Parson Bute],

   "Of every degree,
Ripening early; and ripening late.["]
. . . .
But shake your fruit from the orchard tree,
And the tune of the brook, and the hum of the
   bee,
And the chipmonks chippering every minute,
And the clear sweet note of the gay little linnet,
    And the grass and the flowers,
    And the long summer hours,
And the flavor of sun and breeze, are in it.

(From "Green Apples," by J. T. Trowbridge, poem
published with the engraving, 470–71)

Drawn by Winslow Homer.

"SHE TURNED HER FACE TO THE WINDOW."

6. *She Turned Her Face to the Window,*
illustration for Marion Harland's *Beechdale,* from *The Galaxy,* May 1868, opposite p. 581

Wood engraving, 4⅞ x 7 inches (12.5 x 18 cm). Engraved by E. Sears. 1998.105.107, Gift of Harvey Isbitts

Homer drew five illustrations for the serialized novel *Beechdale,* by Mary Virginia Hawes Terhune (writing under the pseudonym of Marion Harland). The novel is a romantic tale centering on duty, false love, and moral conflict in a town called Beechdale. In this engraving the young heroine, Jessie, is depicted as she is introduced at the opening of the book, recovering from a sprained foot. She dreamily listens to the voice of Roy Fordham as it is carried by the breeze through the open window, until she is interrupted from her happy reveries about Roy (to whom she is secretly engaged) by the unexpected arrival of his cousin, Orrin Wyllys. After polite conversation, "she turned her face to the window," drawn by her greater interest in following Roy's activity. Rather than fully delineating the scene of Orrin's visit, Homer suggested Jessie's wandering thoughts, emphasizing mood in favor of narrated events. In this connection, Homer's drawing forecast his paintings of the early 1870s featuring contemplative women positioned near windows, symbolizing access to the world beyond domesticity.   —BDG

"YOU ARE REALLY PICTURESQUE, MY LOVE."—Page 720.

7. *"You Are Really Picturesque, My Love,"*
illustration for Marion Harland's *Beechdale,* from *The Galaxy,* June 1868, p. 718

Wood engraving, 4¼ x 6⅞ inches (12.2 x 17.6 cm). 1998.105.108, Gift of Harvey Isbitts

As *Beechdale* unfolds, it is discovered that the wife of Septimus Baxter, president of Marion College in the not-too-distant town of Hamilton, is the first cousin of Jessie's long-dead mother, who had suffered from emotional frailty (possibly the nineteenth-century women's malady neurasthenia). The reader is introduced to the Baxters in the novel's only humorous passage, in which the exacting Mrs. Baxter (whose specialty is etiquette, or "Manner") tries to coax her rumpled husband into improving his posture and dressing in a way more appropriate to his position in the community. As the text describes him, "[his] trousers bagged at the knees, and his coats hung in loose folds straight down from his shoulder-blades, on the very day they left the tailor's shop; [they] were shabby within twenty-four hours." Partly from dismay and partly to encourage him to relinquish his lackadaisical habits, the autocratic Mrs. Baxter declares, "You are really picturesque, my love." Homer's depiction of the scene reveals the care he took in achieving the physical and psychological type of each character; he literally divided the composition according to their respective attributes. Mrs. Baxter is shown in strict profile and sits in a straight-backed chair, signaling the rigidity of her personality and habits. Her husband, on the other hand, is slumped in an easy chair, a vision of relaxation and impervious to his wife's demands.

Orrin Wyllys is acquainted with the Baxters and takes it upon himself to arrange for the high-strung Jessie to spend some time with them. He hopes to keep her occupied for the duration of his cousin Roy's long absence in quest of professional advancement.   —BDG

Drawn by Winslow Homer.
JESSIE REMAINED ALONE AT THE TABLE.—Page 78.

8. *Jessie Remained Alone at the Table,*
illustration for Marion Harland's *Beechdale,* from *The Galaxy,* July 1868, opposite p. 68

Wood engraving, 7 x 5¼ inches (17.9 x 14.7 cm). 1998.105.110, Gift of Harvey Isbitts

Jessie visits the Baxters to revive family connections. While she is staying with them, she is embraced by local society, especially the Provost family. Mr. Provost encouraged modern forms of recreation for his daughters, such as billiard playing. On one afternoon at the Provost home, Jessie overhears idle gossip concerning a previous marriage engagement that her beloved Roy Fordham had broken. The information unsettles her, but she is determined to appear unruffled by the news and pretends to concentrate on her game. Despite Jessie's isolation at the billiard table, Homer deftly insinuated the idea of her attentiveness to the young women's conversation by positioning her bright, crisply defined head on the same compositional line occupied by the less distinctly rendered heads of the group behind her. This scene sets the tone for the remainder of the chapter, in which the impressionable Jessie is increasingly attracted to Orrin (her protector in Roy's absence) and wrestles with her conflicting feelings for the two men. What the naive Jessie does not realize, however, is that Orrin's character is shallow and his attentions are mere flirtation. —BDG

"ORRIN, MAKE HASTE, I AM PERISHING!"—Page 228.

9. *"Orrin, Make Haste, I Am Perishing!"* illustration for Marion Harland's *Beechdale,* from *The Galaxy,* August 1868, opposite p. 217

Wood engraving, 4¾ x 7 inches (12.2 x 17.9 cm). 1998.105.115, Gift of Harvey Isbitts

Jessie clings desperately to a tree trunk in the chill waters of a stream into which she plunged when the rail of an old wooden bridge collapsed under her weight. Moments earlier she had contemplated the bleakness of her existence—betrothed to one man (Roy) and attracted to his cousin (Orrin). Now, however, she realizes how precious life is and prays for Orrin to rescue her. The view of the rural countryside seen through the arched bridge underscores the remoteness of the area and the equally remote probability of rescue by a chance passerby. Homer concentrated on Jessie's feelings of hopelessness as the cold water slowly numbs her grip. The emotional oppressiveness is heightened by the shape of the bridge, which confines her within the compositional space. As in later works, Homer lavished a great deal of attention here on purely abstract passages of the composition such as the reflective and transparent properties of the water. Jessie's prayers are answered, and Orrin does, indeed, pull her from the cold stream. The two then acknowledge their mutual attraction, but out of duty to Roy, Jessie struggles to deny her emotions. —BDG

Drawn by Winslow Homer.

"I CANNOT! IT WOULD BE A SIN! A FEARFUL SIN!"—Page 354.

10. *"I Cannot! It Would Be a Sin! A Fearful Sin!"*
illustration for Marion Harland's *Beechdale,* from *The Galaxy,* August 1868, opposite p. 341

Wood engraving, 7 x 5 inches (17.9 x 12.8 cm). 1998.105.117, Gift of Harvey Isbitts

Ignorant of Jessie's conflicted feelings, her dying father insists that she and Roy honor their vows to marry. Here Roy has just restated his love for Jessie, and she sinks to the floor, overcome by her feelings about the sinfulness of entering into a loveless marriage. Although the imagery of a woman prostrate at the feet of a man would have been familiar to Homer's viewers (for it echoes the Victorian iconography attached to the narrative of the "fallen woman"), Homer added a twist to common expectations by reversing the placement of the more sympathetic character within the composition. The novel ends, if not happily, at least properly. Jessie abides by her father's last wish and marries Roy, whose patience and understanding bode well for their future. Orrin is revealed as the shallow cad he really is when he marries the rich young woman whose billiard-room gossip shook Jessie's faith in Roy at the outset.

As suggested by these five illustrations, Homer chose to portray episodes that genuinely amplify the text by focusing on pivotal states of mind and conditions of character. With the exception of the first image *(She Turned Her Face to the Window),* however, the illustrations fail to convey the more intriguing narrative ambiguities that permeate his contemporaneous paintings. Nonetheless, this type of freelance work probably sharpened Homer's own sensibilities regarding contemporary life and mores—all of which doubtless fed his independent explorations of female interiority.   —BDG

"ALL IN THE GAY AND GOLDEN WEATHER."

11. "All in the Gay and Golden Weather," from *Appletons' Journal of Literature, Science and Art,* June 12, 1869, cover

Wood engraving, 5½ x 6½ inches (14.1 x 16.7 cm). Engraved by James L. Langridge. 1998.105.128, Gift of Harvey Isbitts

Alice Cary's "All in the Gay and Golden Weather" exemplifies the popular type of moralizing, pedestrian rhymes that often told of the pitfalls of romance governed solely by the heat of passion. Homer's drawing accompanied Cary's verses, which establish, at length, a metaphor between a flower turning its face to the burning sun and a woman who submits to the ardor of her suitor; in the end, both will be burned. Homer's image seems to refer to the opening stanza (which appears under it): "All in the gay and golden weather, / Two fair travellers, maid and man, / Sailed in a birchen boat together, / And sailed the way that the river ran: / The sun was low, not set, and the west / Was colored like a robin's breast." However, the emotional tension between the two figures (whose gazes fail to meet) alerts the viewer to the darker aspects of the poem's theme, for, as the boat "sailed the way the river ran," the heedless couple is carried by the current, unaware that they head for a nearby waterfall:

Close on the precipice rang the ditty,
But they looked behind them, and not
before,
And went down singing their doleful pity
About the blossom safe on the shore—
"There is danger, danger! Frail one, list!"
Backward whirled in the whirling mist. (322)

Although David Tatham has suggested that the poem was written to complement this image, such a chronology seems unlikely here.[1] It is difficult to suppose that Homer would have independently created what is in itself a rather prosaic image and one so unlike his current work in oils or, for that matter, his other illustrations—especially when his energies were so clearly focused on advancing his reputation as a painter.

—BDG

1. David Tatham, *Winslow Homer and the Illustrated Book* (Syracuse, N.Y.: Syracuse University Press, 1992), 98.

Drawn by Winslow Homer.

"COME !"—p. 310.

12. *"Come!"* illustration for Annie Edwards's *Susan Fielding,* from *The Galaxy,* September 1869, opposite p. 293

Wood engraving, 4⅞ x 6⅞ inches (12.5 x 17.6 cm). 1998.105.135, Gift of Harvey Isbitts

Homer was commissioned to create five drawings for the serialized novel *Susan Fielding* by Annie Edwards, a popular and prolific English writer of romantic potboilers. The first of the group shows Susan Fielding on the train departing London for the ferry to France. Orphaned and impoverished, she is on her way to live in Brittany in the care of an elderly uncle. Rooted in contrasts between city and country, wealth and poverty, virtue and duplicity, the novel is full of romantic intrigue. Before leaving her country village, Susan had hastily and unwisely committed herself to marry the churlish Tom Collinson. In the meantime, she had met the artistic and sensitive George Blake, only to discover that she has feelings for him, which to her delight and dismay are reciprocated. (Collinson's business travels to New Zealand keep him out of the picture—a convenient plot device frequently used in such Victorian tales of romantic conflict.) In this illustration George sees Susan off to France, pressing her to allow him to visit her over the summer. Confused, she wavers between duty to Collinson and her desire to see George. As the train pulls away, "Tom Collinson, her engagement, everything in the wide world but the fact of

losing Blake, fades from her, and this poor little daughter of Eve puts her head through the window, and in her clear, girl's voice, cries, 'Come!'" (310).

David Tatham has noted the awkward disjunction of scale between Susan's figure and George's, theorizing that it may be attributed to Homer's habit of using stock figures from previous drawings, which fail to achieve compositional unity when brought together.[1] Although Homer often did repeat figures throughout his art, it is also possible that the spatial dislocation evident here was intended to enhance the narrative, for it invokes the idea of the moving train and heightens the sense of suspense leading up to Susan's impetuous cry from the window. It is also clear, however, that Homer made no effort to create an image of the countrified Susan as she is described in the book. Instead, she is a product of his imagination, appearing as a stylishly dressed young woman whose clothing suggests a worldliness that contradicts what the reader is told of her youth, poverty, and innocence.

—BDG

1. David Tatham, *Winslow Homer and the Illustrated Book* (Syracuse, N.Y.: Syracuse University Press, 1992), 83.

Drawn by Winslow Homer.
" I CALL THEM MY CHILDREN—TO MYSELF, SUSAN."—p. 443.

13. *"I Call Them My Children—to Myself, Susan,"* illustration for Annie Edwards's
Susan Fielding, from *The Galaxy,* October 1869, opposite p. 437

Wood engraving, 7 x 4 ½ inches (18 x 11.6 cm). 1998.105.137, Gift of Harvey Isbitts

In this more literal (and more prosaic) illustration of the text, the second drawing of the group, Susan's depiction conforms to the descriptions of her in the novel. Susan's frail Uncle Adam shows her his garden behind the small cottage that is now her home in a rural French village. It is the only spot of beauty in his Spartan life, and the brilliant-colored flowers remind Susan of her own lackluster existence. Uncle Adam's loneliness is underscored in his wistful comment about his blooms, "I call them my children—to myself—Susan" (443). The text and the image depend on standardized associations linking floral delicacy and womanhood, and thus establish the notion that Susan is also a fragile beauty who must be carefully tended. Just a short distance away from her uncle's enclosed garden is a fashionable summer resort, where Susan's greedy, willful friend Portia Ffrench (*sic*) and her entourage stay. Portia's manipulations bring Susan into her sphere, complicating the girl's feelings about loyalty and normal youthful desires for pleasure and happiness.

The uneven quality of this set of drawings suggests Homer's disinterest in the commission. He may have been bored with an undeniably tedious text and resented the time and energy that such jobs took away from his work in oil and watercolor. The fact that he was not the sole illustrator assigned to the project (Sol Eytinge drew the third and fourth images for the serial) may have diluted any initial enthusiasm he may have felt, or conversely, Eytinge's participation might have been the result of Homer's reluctance to continue with the work. —BDG

Drawn by Winslow Homer.
WEARY AND DISSATISFIED WITH EVERYTHING.—p. 590.

14. *"Weary and Dissatisfied with Everything,"* illustration for Annie Edwards's
Susan Fielding, from *The Galaxy,* November 1869, opposite p. 581

Wood engraving, 7⅛ x 4¾ inches (18.3 x 12.2 cm). 1998.105.139, Gift of Harvey Isbitts

The novel's labyrinthine plot shifts from Susan's troubles to those of her cunning, socially adept friend Portia. Portia's life at the French resort grows even more complicated, for both her suitor Josselin (whom she has promised her wealthy grandmother never to see again) and George Blake (whose affection for the engaged Susan is not publicly declared) are in attendance. Unexpectedly, her attractive, older cousin John Dysart arrives. It was Dysart who had taught her the ways of the world years earlier, and Portia's emotional dependence on him has not lessened. On the walkway near the casino, she pours out her heart to him about her troubles. He responds: "Weary and dissatisfied with everything! You used to tell me just the same story when you were sixteen." This is said at the moment that Susan, Blake, and Josselin suddenly come upon them:

John Dysart, who was leaning with consider-able earnestness of manner over his companion, had his head turned aside. Portia's face—the beautiful, discontented face which even at this moment Blake could not help crediting with so much more emotion than its owner was capa-ble of feeling—was distinctly outlined against the opal background of still sea. (590)

Although Homer did not convey the scene in strict detail, his depiction of the exchange between Portia and Dysart accurately captures the mood of the text. What is more, the episode permitted him to pursue his customary interest in portraying elegantly costumed women; and in this instance, the modish attire harmoniously coincided with a character defined by her material desires.   —BDG

Drawn by Winslow Homer.

IN CAME A STORM OF WIND, RAIN AND SPRAY—AND PORTIA.—p. 739.

15. *In Came a Storm of Wind, Rain and Spray—and Portia,* illustration for
Annie Edwards's *Susan Fielding,* from *The Galaxy,* December 1869, opposite p. 725

Wood engraving, 6½ x 4½ inches (16.2 x 11.6 cm). 1998.105.141, Gift of Harvey Isbitts

As a ploy to spend more time with Josselin, her forbidden lover, Portia arranges a boating party, which is to include Susan, George Blake, her cousin Dysart, and another couple. For various reasons, all but Josselin beg off the trip, and Portia whiles away the day in the boat alone with him. As evening falls, a raging storm hits, and the two are caught in its fury. Portia's Aunt Jemima has spent anxious hours waiting for her niece's return. The scene portrayed here shows Portia, breathless from a farewell kiss from Josselin, confronted by her irate aunt, who witnessed the kiss and mistakenly believed her niece's companion to be Dysart. Again, Homer took obvious delight in drawing Portia's fashionable costume. The image roughly echoes his earlier treatment of the character in its paralleling of interior thought and mode of attire. The gusts of wind make the voluminous material difficult to control, and the fabric takes on irregular, angular shapes that reinforce the idea of Portia's emotional agitation.
—BDG

GEORGE BLAKE'S LETTER.—p. 258.

16. *George Blake's Letter*, illustration for Annie Edwards's *Susan Fielding*, from *The Galaxy*, January 1870, frontispiece

Wood engraving, 6½ x 4½ inches (16.7 x 11.6 cm). 1998.105.142, Gift of Harvey Isbitts

Shortly after the death of her kindly uncle, Susan learns that her fiancé, Tom Collinson, is returning to claim her as his bride. Sadly, she reads a letter from her true love, George Blake, in which he entreats her for one final meeting before she marries. The crumpled letter from her future sister-in-law detailing the arrangements for the wedding lies on the window ledge beside her. Throughout the whole of her friendship with George, Susan has remained true to Collinson and intends to remain so, despite the fact that she does not love him. The novel ends happily, however, with Portia and Josselin married and wealthy, and Susan and George destined to be together because Collinson's shady past is revealed. Of the five illustrations that Homer produced for this novel, only this one approaches his work in oils in terms of its pictorial strength and depth of feeling, and indeed, it bears striking similarity to a number of his canvases and watercolors depicting solitary women.

—BDG

"Thou shalt not covet thy neighbor's house, thou shalt not covet thy neighbor's wife, nor his servant, nor his maid, nor his ox, nor his ass, nor any thing that is his."

"Lord, have mercy upon us, and write all these thy laws in our hearts, we beseech thee."

17. *Tenth Commandment,* from *Harper's Weekly,* March 12, 1870, cover

Wood engraving, 10¾ x 9 inches (27.4 x 23 cm). 1998.105.146, Gift of Harvey Isbitts

This illustration of the biblical Tenth Commandment cast in contemporaneous terms seems a curious image for the cover of a weekly magazine with a general readership. No reference explaining the reasoning behind its commission has been located. The choice of subject, however, may have been related indirectly to the political scandals gripping the nation at the time— one of which centered on the presidency of Ulysses S. Grant. Shaken by corruption, the administration yielded the term "Grantism," which came to encompass all manner of political corruption, avarice, and cronyism. Although the *Harper's Weekly* issue for which Homer's *Tenth Commandment* was the cover contained an editorial in defense of Grant, the image may have been intended as a moralizing lesson to those whose actions had weakened the presidency.

—BDG

WAITING FOR A BITE.—[DRAWN BY WINSLOW HOMER.]

18. *Waiting for a Bite,* from *Harper's Weekly,* August 22, 1874, p. 693

Wood engraving, 9 x 13 ¹¹⁄₁₆ inches (23 x 35 cm). 1998.105.191, Gift of Harvey Isbitts

In the 1860s, while living in New York City, Homer traveled to the wilderness in surrounding areas to camp, fish, and paint, and by 1870 he had started visiting the Adirondacks. His hunting and fishing activities there later became the subject of many watercolors and oil paintings. In the summer of 1874, when he made this illustration, Homer is known to have spent time with friends at Keene Valley in the Adirondacks. The image, with its bucolic depiction of boys whiling away the hours fishing, reflects post–Civil War attitudes that valued childhood innocence and play. The engraving appeared without any accompanying text, but it finds echoes in a scene in *Tom Sawyer* (written just two years later), when Tom lies in the quiet of the forested wilderness: "[N]ature lay in a trance that was broken by no sound but the occasional far-off hammering of a wood-pecker. . . . It must be very peaceful, he thought, to lie and slumber and dream forever and ever."[1] Homer's image also calls to mind the novel's celebration of the bounty and wonder of the wilderness where Tom, Huck, and Joe find refuge:

> *Huck found a spring of clear cold water close by, and the boys made cups of broad oak or hickory leaves, and felt that water, sweetened with such a wildwood charm as that, would be a good enough substitute for coffee. While Joe was slicing bacon for breakfast, Tom and Huck asked him to hold on a minute; they stepped to a promising nook in the river-bank and threw in their lines; almost immediately they had reward. Joe had not time to get impatient before they were back again with some handsome bass, a couple of sun-perch and a small catfish.*[2]

—MSK

1. Mark Twain, *The Adventures of Tom Sawyer* (1876; reprint, New York: Harper & Brothers, 1903), 91–92.
2. Ibid., 146–47.

CIVIL WAR ILLUSTRATIONS

The Civil War began on April 12, 1861, when Confederate forces fired on Fort Sumter, South Carolina. Homer had been working for *Harper's Weekly* for three years and had just been in Washington, D.C., the previous month covering Lincoln's inauguration. By May he was illustrating Civil War news from New York State. In October *Harper's Weekly* sent him with General George McClellan's Army of the Potomac to the front. Homer did not see any action and was back home with his family on October 21.

On March 17, 1862, General McClellan began moving his army toward Richmond, having decided with President Lincoln that the best chance for a quick resolution of the war was to capture the Confederate capital. Homer spent about two months at the front in Virginia, making drawings of the battles that he witnessed, as well as camp life in general. By June 7 he had been home long enough for his mother to write to Arthur, his younger brother, "Winslow went to the war front of Yorktown and camped out about two months. He suffered much, was without food 3 days at a time & all in camp either died or were carried away with typhoid fever—plug tobacco & coffee was [*sic*] the Staples. . . . He came home so changed that his best friends did not know him, but is well & all right now."[1]

The war raged on for three more years until April 9, 1865, when General Robert E. Lee surrendered at Appomattox Court House. Homer may have gone to the front one more time, in May 1864, to witness the Battle of the Wilderness in Fredericksburg, Virginia, but this visit has not been explicitly documented. The images that Homer made of the war after his visit in spring 1862 were most likely made from memory. His exemplary ability to depict not only the war years, but also the effects of the war upon a tired and torn nation attempting to put itself together afterward, was conveyed by a contemporary reviewer: "It is invigorating to find boldness and truth amidst the trivial and false. In the works of Winslow Homer we have a direct style and faithful observation of nature. . . . Welcome this hearty energy of life."[2]   —MSK

---

1. Quoted in Gordon Hendricks, *The Life and Work of Winslow Homer* (New York: Harry N. Abrams, 1979), 50.

2. "National Academy of Design/Fortieth Annual Exhibition. Concluding Article," *Evening Post*, May 31, 1865, quoted in Marc Simpson et al., *Winslow Homer: Paintings of the Civil War*, exh. cat. (San Francisco: The Fine Arts Museums of San Francisco and Bedford Arts, Publishers, 1988), 15.

HARPER'S WEEKLY.

A JOURNAL OF CIVILIZATION.

VOL. V.—No. 220.] NEW YORK, SATURDAY, MARCH 16, 1861. [PRICE FIVE CENTS.

Entered according to Act of Congress, in the Year 1861, by Harper & Brothers, in the Clerk's Office of the District Court for the Southern District of New York.

THE INAUGURAL PROCESSION AT WASHINGTON PASSING THE GATE OF THE CAPITOL GROUNDS.—FROM A SKETCH BY OUR SPECIAL ARTIST.—[SEE PAGE 165.]

19. *The Inaugural Procession at Washington Passing the Gate of the Capitol Grounds,*
from *Harper's Weekly,* March 16, 1861, cover

Wood engraving, 11 x 9⅛ inches (27.9 x 23.2 cm). 1998.105.50, Gift of Harvey Isbitts

Abraham Lincoln was inaugurated as president on March 4, 1861. The procession was supposed to begin at 9 A.M. but did not get under way until much later because, as noted in the *Harper's* article, President Buchanan was "still in his chamber at the Capitol signing bills. It was not till ten minutes past twelve that he left the Capitol. He drove rapidly to the White House, entered an open barouche with servants in livery, and proceeded to Willard's [Hotel, where Lincoln was staying]. There the President-elect, and Senators Pearce and Baker of the Committee of Arrangements, entered the carriage, and a few minutes before one the procession began to move" ("The Inauguration," 165). These are the people whom Homer depicted in the carriage as it proceeded on its way to the Capitol for the inauguration ceremonies.   —MSK

20. *The Songs of the War,* from *Harper's Weekly,* November 23, 1861, pp. 744–45

Wood engraving, 13⅞ x 20⅛ inches (35.3 x 51.1 cm). 1998.105.63, Gift of Harvey Isbitts

With the war only seven months old, hopes were still running high that a Union victory was within reach, and one sees these enthusiastic sentiments in the depictions of Homer's figures. The largest amount of space in this image was given to "Glory Hallelujah," the popular refrain from the song "John Brown's Body," to which so many of the Union soldiers marched. (Shortly after Homer's illustration appeared, "John Brown's Body" was given new words and renamed "The Battle Hymn of the Republic.") Homer made this illustration in the autumn of 1861, when there was discussion in the press about a national hymn appropriate to the temper of the times. A writer for *Harper's Weekly* declared: "And when . . . the spirit of the country is as military as for many years it is likely to be, then the 'tune' which is most popular, and which is universally played by all its bands, at all its ports, and along all its lines, and which is associated with some act of heroic daring and triumph, will doubtless become the melody of a national hymn."[1]   —MSK

---

1. "National Hymns," *Harper's Weekly,* November 16, 1861, 723.

A BIVOUAC FIRE ON THE POTOMAC.

21. *A Bivouac Fire on the Potomac*, from *Harper's Weekly*, December 21, 1861, pp. 808–9

Wood engraving, 13⅞ x 20¼ inches (35.3 x 51.5 cm). 1998.105.64, Gift of Harvey Isbitts

Homer had briefly accompanied the Union forces at the front in Virginia in October 1861 as a special war correspondent for *Harper's Weekly*. The Union army had just been defeated at the First Battle of Bull Run and was then stationed under General George Brinton McClellan just outside Washington, D.C., as the forces were being reorganized. While there, Homer saw no fighting but made many sketches of life in camp. *A Bivouac Fire on the Potomac* and other engravings that he did in this period were based on these earlier drawings of soldiers and their activities.

—MSK

HARPER'S WEEKLY.
A JOURNAL OF CIVILIZATION.

Vol. VI.—No. 281.] NEW YORK, SATURDAY, MAY 17, 1862. [SINGLE COPIES SIX CENTS.
[$2 50 PER YEAR IN ADVANCE.

Entered according to Act of Congress, in the Year 1862, by Harper & Brothers, in the Clerk's Office of the District Court for the Southern District of New York.

REBELS OUTSIDE THEIR WORKS AT YORKTOWN RECONNOITRING WITH DARK LANTERNS.—SKETCHED BY MR. WINSLOW HOMER.—[SEE PAGE 315.]

22. *Rebels Outside Their Works at Yorktown—Reconnoitring [sic] with Dark Lanterns,* from *Harper's Weekly,* May 17, 1862, cover

Wood engraving, 10⅞ x 9¼ inches (27.7 x 23.6 cm). 1998.105.69, Gift of Harvey Isbitts

In the spring of 1862, General McClellan, commander of the Union forces, fortified his position in order to lay siege to Yorktown, where he believed he could defeat the rebel forces. There never was a battle at Yorktown, however, because the Confederates held off the Union army long enough to fortify Richmond, the Southern capital, and then retreated. In May, McClellan wrote his wife, "It would have been easy for me to have sacrificed 10,000 lives in taking Yorktown, and I presume the world would have thought it more brilliant. I am content with what I have done."[1] Without any battle activity to report at this time, some of the journals, including *Harper's Weekly,* had illustrated the Union encampments; these issues were confiscated by the War Department, which did not want details of the Union sites published. Subsequently, more generalized depictions of war activity at the front, like this one, appeared.

—MSK

1. Letter of May 8, 1862, quoted in *Civil War: The Years Asunder* (Waukesha, Wis.: Country Beautiful, 1973), 74.

NEWS FROM THE WAR.—[Drawn by our Special Artist, Mr. Winslow Homer.]

23. *News from the War,* from *Harper's Weekly,* June 14, 1862, pp. 376–77

Wood engraving, 13⅛ x 20⅜ inches (34 x 51.7 cm). 1998.105.73, Gift of Harvey Isbitts

In this issue of *Harper's Weekly,* the editors wrote:

News of the war! We all live on it. . . . Little she recks, whose face is buried in her handkerchief in an agony of anguish, of the utter discomfiture of the rebels! . . . And then there is the news of Union victories, conveyed through trumpet-tongued rumor, to gallant Unionists in prison in the South . . . ; to wounded men in hospital and in sorrow,
whose pains seem less acute and whose blood courses more freely as they realize that the cause in which they suffered has received new lustre; to soldiers in the camp, who hear, with half-suppressed jealousy, of glories they did not share. . . . The only thing which thrills every heart nowadays is the News of the War. Mr. Homer, we think, has done justice to this subject. ("News of the War," 378)

THE WAR FOR THE UNION 1862—A CAVALRY CHARGE.

24. *The War for the Union 1862—A Cavalry Charge,* from *Harper's Weekly,* July 5, 1862, pp. 424–25

Wood engraving, 13⅝ x 20⅝ inches (34.8 x 52.4 cm). 1998.105.74, Gift of Harvey Isbitts

In late June and early July 1862, General McClellan was preparing to take Richmond, the Confederate capital. Believing that he lacked manpower, he did not capitalize upon his successes in the area, but instead chose to secure his retreat and withdraw his army up the James River, where they would be safe but still able to threaten Richmond. Some in the North were so assured that the war would be won quickly by the Union that an editorial in this issue of *Harper's Weekly* proclaimed, "Most of the correspondents appear calmly confident of the result. The army is in such splendid condition [and] . . . it is so thoroughly impressed with belief in its own success, that officers, men, and newspaper writers all predict a triumph" ("Before Richmond," 418). Nevertheless, some believe that this image is idealized, because the cavalry actually consisted largely of farmers and city dwellers who had little experience with fast horses. One Union soldier wrote in October 1863: "[W]e have considerable cavalry with us but they are the laughing stock of the army and the boys poke all kinds of fun at them. I really have as yet to see or hear of their doing anything of much credit."[1]   —MSK

1. From Philip Smith diary, October 22, 1863, as cited by Bell Irvin Wiley, *The Life of Billy Yank* (New York: Bobbs-Merrill, 1951), 327, quoted by Christopher Kent Wilson in Marc Simpson et al., *Winslow Homer: Paintings of the Civil War,* exh. cat. (San Francisco: The Fine Arts Museums of San Francisco and Bedford Arts, Publishers, 1988), 42.

OUR WOMEN AND THE WAR.—[See Page 570.]

25. *Our Women and the War*, from *Harper's Weekly*, September 6, 1862, pp. 568–69

Wood engraving, 13 ½ x 20 ½ inches (34.4 x 52.1 cm). 1998.105.76, Gift of Harvey Isbitts

Women's efforts during the war were directed at assisting and supporting the men's fighting efforts. They ministered to dying men, wrote home for the sick, made clothes for the troops, and washed their clothes. As was noted in the accompanying text, the illustration demonstrates "what women may do towards relieving the sorrows and pains of the soldier.... The moral of the picture is sufficiently obvious; there is no woman who can not in some way do something to help the army.... This war of ours has developed scores of Florence Nightingales, whose names no one knows, but whose reward, in the soldier's gratitude and Heaven's approval, is the highest guerdon woman can ever win." ("Our Women and the War," 570)   —MSK

THE ARMY OF THE POTOMAC—A SHARP-SHOOTER ON PICKET DUTY.—[FROM A PAINTING BY W. HOMER, ESQ.]

26. *The Army of the Potomac—A Sharp-Shooter on Picket Duty,* from *Harper's Weekly,* November 15, 1862, p. 724

Wood engraving, 9 1/16 x 13 5/8 inches (23 x 34.7 cm). 1998.160.10, Gift of Harvey Isbitts

As a result of the development in the 1860s of a far more accurate telescopic sight, sharpshooters were first used extensively in the Civil War. Perched high up in trees on the front lines, the sharpshooter would sit quietly for hours waiting for the moment when he could fire upon the enemy. A contemporary account noted:

> [S]ome of those Yankee sharpshooters . . . had little telescopes on their rifles that would fetch a man up close until he seemed to be only 100 yards away from the muzzle. I've seen them pick a man off who was a mile away. They could hit so far you couldn't hear the report of a gun. You wouldn't have any idea anybody was in sight of you, and all of a sudden, with everything as silent as the grave and not a sound of a gun, here would come . . . one of those "forced" balls and cut a hole clear through you.[1]

The devastating effect of sharpshooters owed more to the feeling of vulnerability that they created in the enemy front lines than to the magnitude of casualties they actually inflicted. —MSK

---

1. Quoted in C. A. Stevens, *Berdan's United States Sharpshooters in the Army of the Potomac, 1861–1865* (Dayton, Ohio: Morningside Press, 1972), 462–63.

THANKSGIVING IN CAMP.

27. *Thanksgiving in Camp*, from *Harper's Weekly*, November 29, 1862, p. 764

Wood engraving, 9 x 13¼ inches (23 x 35.1 cm). 1998.105.77, Gift of Harvey Isbitts

In November 1862, when this image was published, Homer was in New York after having spent two months at the front the previous spring. While he was with the forces of the Peninsular Campaign, he saw little fighting but did experience the siege on Yorktown. Homer stayed near Yorktown with his friend Colonel Francis Channing Barlow, who would later be depicted as the Union officer in Homer's 1866 painting *Prisoners from the Front*. About their time spent together, Barlow wrote to his brother Edward: "I have enjoyed . . . Homer's visit exceedingly. . . . I have not laughed so much since I left home. . . . They [Homer and Barlow's brother Richard] have done the cooking."[1] This illustration of Thanksgiving in the camp obviously was imaginary, for Homer spent Thanksgiving with his family in 1862.

—MSK

1. Francis Barlow to Edward Barlow, April 18, 1862, cited in David Tatham, *Winslow Homer Prints from "Harper's Weekly,"* exh. cat. (Glens Falls, Rochester, and Hamilton, N.Y.: Hyde Collection, Margaret Woodbury Strong Museum, and Gallery Association of New York State, 1979), 8.

THE APPROACH OF THE BRITISH PIRATE "ALABAMA."

28. *The Approach of the British Pirate "Alabama,"*
from *Harper's Weekly,* April 25, 1863, p. 268

Wood engraving, 13¾ x 9⅛ inches (35 x 23.2 cm). 1998.105.81, Gift of Harvey Isbitts

The article that this illustration accompanied began, "It is not to be disguised that our relations with Great Britain have reached a most critical pass." In support of the Confederates, British cruisers (including the *Alabama*) not only were running the Union blockade imposed on the Confederate coastline but also were preying upon Union merchant vessels. The article continued: "Every British dock-yard is now engaged in building steamers to capture and burn our merchantmen, to run our blockade, and to bombard our defenseless sea-board cities. . . . [T]he merchants, shipbuilders, and newspapers of England all claim the right of furnishing the rebels with a navy, and denounce us furiously for objecting to their conduct. . . . There has never been a time when hatred of the English was so deep or so wide-spread as it is at present" ("Our Relations with Great Britain," 258). Homer depicts the alarm of the Union ship's passengers as they are being approached by the British vessel, the *Alabama.*

           —MSK

29. *"Any Thing for Me, If You Please?" Post-Office of the Brooklyn Fair in Aid of the Sanitary Commission,* from *Harper's Weekly,* March 5, 1864, p. 156

Wood engraving, 13⅜ x 9 inches (34.9 x 23 cm). 1998.105.87, Gift of Harvey Isbitts

There was no Red Cross to aid the soldiers in the Civil War. Instead, the United States Sanitary Commission was created to aid the wounded and their families. The Brooklyn Sanitary Fair, which opened on February 22, 1864, and ran for two weeks, was held in a group of buildings on Montague Street near Court Street. More than $400,000 was raised for the benefit of the war effort through merchandise that was brought in by merchants, farmers, craftsmen, and artists. Another of the fair's fund-raising attractions was a "Post Office" where people could pay to send messages to others at the fair. Usually, appealing young ladies worked in the "Post Office" transcribing and sending the letters—attracting the men, who would go there to flirt with them.

—MSK

THANKSGIVING DAY—HANGING UP THE MUSKET.

30. *Thanksgiving Day—Hanging Up the Musket,*
from *Frank Leslie's Illustrated Newspaper,* December 23, 1865, p. 216

Wood engraving, 14¼ x 9¼ inches (36.2 x 23.5 cm). 1998.105.93, Gift of Harvey Isbitts

With the long Civil War finally over, veterans could hang up their guns as trophies of battle. Following some controversy, President Andrew Johnson signed a bill in the spring of 1865 allowing soldiers to retain their firearms, recognizing that ownership of these guns was a source of pride. In this engraving, the broken gun of 1776, symbolizing the shattered promises of the Revolutionary War, hangs above the new firearm of the most recent war. The image accompanied an article that declared, "[N]ow we have peace smiling over all the land, and its promise for many years to come. . . . Our soldiers have hung up their bruised arms for monuments . . . if the great moral example of the past five years is to have any effect on the world—until all fall with rust on the peaceful hearth." ("The Thanksgiving of 1865," 221) —MSK

THE VETERAN IN A NEW FIELD.—FROM A PAINTING BY HOMER.

31. *The Veteran in a New Field,*
from *Frank Leslie's Illustrated Newspaper,* July 13, 1867, p. 268

Wood engraving, 4 3/16 x 6 1/4 inches (10.7 x 15.9 cm). 1998.105.99, Gift of Harvey Isbitts

The account in *Frank Leslie's Illustrated Newspaper* that accompanied this image remarked that "one of the most conclusive evidences of the strength of a republican form of government is the way in which our army has disbanded, each man seeking again the sphere of usefulness which he left only temporarily, to aid the Government in its need. . . . Now, however, that the war is over . . . we can well congratulate ourselves upon the manner in which the veterans have returned to their old fields or sought for new ones, since in this we find one of the surest proofs of the stability of our political system" ("The Veteran in a New Field," 268). The illustration was taken from a painting made only a few months after the South's surrender at Appomattox Court House in April 1865. In addition to the obvious allusion to the war veteran's return to the normalcy of farming in his wheat field, the illustration probably makes reference to a passage from Isaiah 2:4: "And they shall beat their swords into plowshares, and their spears into pruning hooks; nation shall not lift up sword against nation, neither shall they learn war any more." This passage was often cited in contemporary writing, including an editorial in the *New-York Weekly Tribune,* in the fall of 1865, which noted that "we know that thousands upon thousands of our brave soldiers will return gladly to the pruninghooks and plowshares."[1] Another interpretation of the image has posited that as the farmer cuts the grain, so too did the soldier cut down lives of other soldiers in the bloodiest war in United States history.[2] In that reading, the soldier was the reaper of death.   —MSK

1. September 30, 1865, quoted by Nicolai Cikovsky, Jr., in Marc Simpson et al., *Winslow Homer: Paintings of the Civil War,* exh. cat. (San Francisco: The Fine Arts Museums of San Francisco and Bedford Arts, Publishers, 1988), 86.
2. Ibid., 88.

CHILDREN

Attitudes toward childhood changed after the Civil War. Rather than harboring harsh disciplinarian attitudes and treating children as small adults, Americans, shaken by the war, began to see the young years as a time of lost innocence. People were nostalgic for a time that was free from overriding responsibility and, perhaps, simpler and uncorrupted by the midcentury modernity of new machines, use of steam power, and proliferation of printing presses. The barefoot boys found in art and literature with rolled-up, too-short pants and straw hats symbolized this respect for childhood freedom. When Samuel Clemens remarked that he wrote *Adventures of Tom Sawyer* (1876) "to try to pleasantly remind adults of what they once were themselves, and of how they felt and thought and talked," he was only echoing and responding to contemporary sentiments.[1] The carefree boy in the country epitomized how a child should spend his youth, laying a foundation for productive later years in adult society. To this end, Fresh Air Funds were organized in the 1870s to take children away from the city, if even for a short time in the summer, because it was felt that country ways and air could make a lifelong, virtuous impression on their developing personalities.

Periodicals written for children proliferated. One of the most popular was *Our Young Folks,* which published a number of Homer's illustrations, accompanied by poems celebrating carefree childhood amid nature.   —MSK

---

1. Quoted in Sarah Burns, *Pastoral Inventions: Rural Life in Nineteenth-Century American Art and Culture* (Philadelphia: Temple University Press, 1989), 302.

WATCHING THE CROWS.

Drawn by Winslow Homer] [See *Watching the Crows*, page 355.

32. *Watching the Crows*, from *Our Young Folks*, June 1868, p. 355, frontispiece

Wood engraving, 5⅞ x 3¾ inches (15.2 x 9.6 cm). 1998.105.109, Gift of Harvey Isbitts

"Caw, caw!"—*You don't say so!* "Caw,
　caw!"—*What, once more?*
Seems to me I've heard that *observation*
　before,
And I wish you would some *time begin to*
　talk sense.
Come, I've sat here about long enough on
　the fence,
And I'd like you to tell me in confidence
　what
Are your present intentions regarding this
　lot?
Why don't you do something? Or else go
　away?
"Caw, caw!"—*Does that mean that they'll*
　go or they'll stay?
While I'm watching to learn what they're
　up to, I see
That for similar reasons they're just
　watching me!

That's right! Now be brave, and I'll show
　you some fun!
Just light within twenty-nine yards of my
　gun!
I've hunted and hunted you all round the
　lot,
Now you *must come* here, *if you want to*
　be shot!
"Caw, caw!"—*There they go again! Isn't it*
　strange
How they always contrive to keep just out
　of range?
The scamps have been shot at so often, they
　know
To a rod just how far the old shot-gun will
　throw.

(From "Watching the Crows," by J. T. Trowbridge,
poem published with the engraving, 355–56)

SEA-SIDE SKETCHES—A CLAM-BAKE.—[See Page 742.]

33. *Sea-Side Sketches—A Clam Bake,* from *Harper's Weekly,* August 23, 1873, p. 740

Wood engraving, 9 ⅜ x 14 inches (24 x 35.6 cm). 1998.105.177, Gift of Harvey Isbitts

The contemporary account that accompanied this image, which combined elements from Homer's earlier drawings and watercolors, related that "happy are they who can find leisure and opportunity to escape for a few hours from the restraints and heat and dust of the city for a run to the sea-side and indulgence in pleasures. . . . There is something mysterious in the attractions of the sea-side" ("Sea-Side Sketches," 742). A present-day interpretation might find more serious reflections on mortality and survival in the image, in which the boys carrying the pail turn away in disgust from the dead fish in the foreground while those to the right prepare to eat their catch.　　　　　　　　　　—MSK

34. *Snap the Whip*, from *Harper's Weekly,* September 20, 1873, pp. 824–25

Wood engraving, 13¼ x 20¼ inches (35 x 52.8 cm). 1998.105.178, Gift of Harvey Isbitts

The subject of boys at play outside the schoolhouse is a good example of the new post–Civil War attitude that childhood innocence and play were as important as the learning that occurred in the schoolhouse. Some have also suggested that this image, in which the strongest boys hold the center at the hub and the weakest fall off at the outside of the chain, characterizes Winslow Homer's attitudes toward social dynamics.[1]

The article accompanying the engraving quotes "[Thomas] Gray's touching lines," taken from "On a Distant Prospect of Eton College":

> *Gay hope is theirs, by fancy led,*
> *Less pleasing when possessed;*
> *The tear forgot as soon as shed,*
> *The sunshine of the breast.*
> *Theirs buxom health of rosy hue,*
> *Wild wit, invention ever new,*
> *And lively cheer of vigor born;*

> *The thoughtless day, the easy night,*
> *The spirits pure, the slumbers light,*
> *That fly the approach of morn.*

> *Alas! Regardless of their doom,*
> *The little victims play;*
> *No sense have they of ills to come,*
> *No care beyond to-day;*
> *Yet see how all around them wait*
> *The ministers of human fate,*
> *And black Misfortune's baleful train.*
> *Ah! Show them where in ambush stand*
> *To seize their prey, the murderous band;*
> *Ah, tell them they are men!*
> ("Snap-the-Whip," 826)

—MSK

1. Jochen Wierich, "Beyond Innocence: Images of Boyhood from Winslow Homer's First Gloucester Period," in *Winslow Homer in Gloucester* (Chicago: Terra Museum of American Art, 1990), 40.

GLOUCESTER HARBOR.—Drawn by Winslow Homer.—[See Page 854.]

35. *Gloucester Harbor,* from *Harper's Weekly,* September 27, 1873, p. 844

Wood engraving, 9¼ x 14 inches (23.6 x 35.7 cm). 1998.105.179, Gift of Harvey Isbitts

"Its harbor is one of the best on the coast," stated the article that accompanied this illustration ("Gloucester Harbor," 854). Gloucester, which was the first settlement on the North Shore of Massachusetts Bay, lies on the peninsula of Cape Ann, Massachusetts. Accessible to large vessels at all times of the year, Gloucester was a busy seaport known not only for its fishing industry but for its attractiveness to tourists and artists as well. In fact, by the third quarter of the nineteenth century, Gloucester had developed a reputation as a good place for artists to work, having drawn such major American painters as Sanford Gifford, William Trost Richards, and Worthington Whittredge. The artist Fitz Hugh Lang was a native son, having grown up near the waterfront on Cape Ann. Homer spent part of the summer of 1873 in Gloucester, where he lived at the Atlantic Hotel. He passed his days sketching and made his first series of watercolors that summer. It was also during that time that he began his great fascination with the sea.

—MSK

SHIP-BUILDING, GLOUCESTER HARBOR.—DRAWN BY WINSLOW HOMER.—[SEE PAGE 902.]

36. *Ship-Building, Gloucester Harbor,* from *Harper's Weekly*, October 11, 1873, p. 900

Wood engraving, 9⅛ x 13⅝ inches (23.4 x 34.7 cm). 1998.105.180, Gift of Harvey Isbitts

As the men build the big ships in this image, the boys play with their small ones in the foreground. "Gloucester boys who wanted to see what else there was to schooner building would visit a shipyard," one local historian wrote, "and walk ankle deep in chips from the great pine sticks that the skillful axe-men would be hewing into masts for the schooner a-building for some famous skipper of the port."[1] The caption that accompanied this image in *Harper's Weekly* expressed optimism concerning renewed activity in American shipyards. "All along our immense line of coast may be seen indications which awaken the hope that America will soon resume her former supremacy in the building of ships. With her immense resources of coal, iron, and wood, with abundant and intelligent labor at her command, there is no reason why she should not take the lead of all nations in this important branch of industry" ("Ship-Building," 902).

—MSK

1. Jochen Wierich, "Beyond Innocence: Images of Boyhood from Winslow Homer's First Gloucester Period," in *Winslow Homer in Gloucester* (Chicago: Terra Museum of American Art, 1990), 42.

"DAD'S COMING!"—Drawn by Winslow Homer.—[See Poem on Page 970.]

37. *"Dad's Coming!"* from *Harper's Weekly,* November 1, 1873, p. 969

Wood engraving, 9¼ x 13⅝ inches (23.7 x 34.8 cm). 1998.105.181, Gift of Harvey Isbitts

Homer spent the summer of 1873 in Gloucester, Massachusetts. On Sunday, August 24, an especially strong storm claimed nine boats and the lives of 128 men. This image, which Homer first did as a painting, was most likely inspired by that incident. The life of a fisherman was always dangerous, and storms and danger were constantly in the minds of the women and children left behind as the men went to sea to earn a living, as is dramatized by the poem of the same title published with the engraving:

> *Now in the distance a white sail is gleaming,*
> *Flutteringly spread like the wings of a dove;*
> *Nearer and nearer the light breeze is wafting*

> *The wanderer back to the home of his love.*
> *"See! He is coming! Dad's coming! I see*
> *   him!"*
> *Shout, little Johnny! Shout loud in your glee!*
> *Only God heareth the prayer that is*
> *   whispered*
> *For thanks that the sailor comes safely from*
> *   sea.* (970)

One cannot resist speculating that the boy, with his straw hat as a symbol of his innocence, will himself soon be on one of those boats with someone waiting behind watching for him.   —MSK

RAID ON A SAND-SWALLOW COLONY—"HOW MANY EGGS?"—[DRAWN BY WINSLOW HOMER.]

38. *Raid on a Sand-Swallow Colony—"How Many Eggs?"* from *Harper's Weekly,* June 13, 1874, p. 496

Wood engraving, 13 ½ x 9 ⅛ inches (34.3 x 23.3 cm). 1998.105.188, Gift of Harvey Isbitts

No text accompanied this illustration when it appeared in *Harper's Weekly*. A small article in the journal did mention Children's Day festivities in Brooklyn, which featured games, food, and a parade (495). This event and Homer's image exemplify the more indulgent attitudes toward children that prevailed in the United States after the Civil War. In June, with summer coming, children were expected to spend the season playing and enjoying themselves as in Homer's illustration. The deft manner in which he organized the complex composition and arranged the four boys at different levels in the space indicates the work of a mature artist, whose image could stand on its own merits, unaccompanied by any supporting text. The drawing for this illustration was mentioned in a memoir of the young artist James Edward Kelly, who recalled Homer visiting the art director at *Harper's Weekly*: "I have an impression that his drawing was of boys on the face of a cliff after sand swallows' nests."[1]

—MSK

1. James Edward Kelly, "Winslow Homer," James Edward Kelly Papers, Archives of American Art, Smithsonian Institution, Washington, D.C., reel 1876.

GATHERING BERRIES.—[Drawn by Winslow Homer.]

39. *Gathering Berries,* from *Harper's Weekly,* July 11, 1874, p. 584

Wood engraving, 9⅛ x 13½ inches (23.3 x 34.3 cm). 1998.105.189, Gift of Harvey Isbitts

In July 1874 Homer was working in East Hampton, Long Island, the probable setting of this image. While the children have gone out into the field together, they are not interacting with one another. Each seems to be in his or her own private reverie. As noted by the art historian Sarah Burns, writing about children of this time, the mood of this image is very similar to that of a poem written by Lucy Larcom in 1874:

Red lilies blaze out of the thicket
Wild roses blush here and there:

There's sweetness in all the breezes,
There's health in each breath of air.
Hark to the wind in the pine-trees!
Hark to the tinkling rill!
O, pleasant it is a-berrying
In the pastures on the hill![1]

—MSK

1. "Berrying Song," in *Childhood Songs* (1874), facsimile ed. (Great Neck, N.Y.: Granger, 1978), quoted in Sarah Burns, *Pastoral Inventions: Rural Life in Nineteenth-Century American Art and Culture* (Philadelphia: Temple University Press, 1989), 307.

SEESAW—GLOUCESTER, MASSACHUSETTS.—[DRAWN BY WINSLOW HOMER.]

40. *Seesaw—Gloucester, Massachusetts,* from *Harper's Weekly,* September 12, 1874, p. 757

Wood engraving, 9⅛ x 13¾ inches (23.3 x 35 cm). 1998.105.193, Gift of Harvey Isbitts

This illustration is a combination of two earlier watercolors—one that depicted the boys on the seesaw and another that portrayed the three girls playing cat's cradle in the foreground. Homer made no attempt here to change the two compositions so that the boys and girls relate to each other. Such a separation of individuals is not uncommon in Homer's work. The girls are dominated by the boys above them, and yet they also form a base that stabilizes the composition. One wonders whether Homer was commenting on relationships between boys and girls.

—MSK

WOMEN IN MODERN AMERICAN LIFE

Homer's primary identity as a genre specialist—one who concentrates on scenes of everyday life—most likely grew out of early and lengthy experience as an illustrator. His commissions for the popular illustrated weeklies demanded descriptive images that conveyed the immediacy of changing customs, fashions, and values in a manner that could be broadly understood. Such requirements sensitized him to the importance of observable reality, a focus that did not necessarily entail a narrative, but involved keen insight into the signs of change relevant to national experience.

Major changes were wrought in the lives of women as a result of the Civil War, making female activity a rich reservoir of subject matter for Homer and his contemporaries. Prior to 1860, most American women's lives were framed by work within the home—either maintenance of the family or piecework conducted on the domestic front and sold on the regional market. The war spurred industrialization, bringing changes in the shape of the workforce, new leisure habits, and new markets for mass-produced goods. By featuring women going about their daily lives in his illustrations, Homer was able to incorporate references to these social and economic shifts in a way that was almost universally recognizable to his audience. Thus, for example, his scenes of women engaging in outdoor sports like skating or croquet not only pointed to the newly popular craze for health-promoting exercise, but also referred to new venues for social interaction between the sexes and the fashions recommended for such activities. Similarly, the growing contrasts between city and country life were played out in the "types" of women Homer portrayed: the hardworking farm girl; the city woman with her highly regulated social life; the factory worker; and the art student, schoolmistress, and others of the emerging class of women who aspired to professional status in previously male-dominated pursuits. This contrast of types is evident throughout Homer's work.

—BDG

HARPER'S WEEKLY.

329

MAY 22, 1858.]

THE BOSTON COMMON.

41. *The Boston Common,* from *Harper's Weekly,* May 22, 1858, p. 329

Wood engraving, 9 ⅛ x 13 ¾ inches (23.3 x 35.1 cm). 1998.105.15, Gift of Harvey Isbitts

This early engraving was executed while Homer still resided in his native Boston. Then, as now, Bostonians were justifiably proud of the Common, as was expressed in the *Harper's* article that this illustration accompanied: "Take the Common as it stands, with the fountain, and the elm, and the historical associations—and I defy the world to produce its equal." The unknown writer's argument in proclaiming Boston superior to New York City rested largely on the pleasures afforded by the Common: "The Common is a wild expanse of ground—much larger and more airy than any place you have in New York. . . . For children . . . it is a delightful place; and when I think of the agonies the poor little things endure, pent up in your wretched steaming city [New York], during the hot months of summer, and of the dangers of your parks and squares, infested as they are by the worst class of people, I confess I envied the Bostonian mothers their advantages" ("Life in Boston," 328). As a venue for fashionable promenades and health-inducing recreation for children, the Common was a valuable asset in the competitive battles waged among American cities, enabling Boston to outstrip New York in this category until Central Park was closer to completion. Homer encompassed these ideal features of the Common in his drawing, creating a genteel impression of contemporary Boston life as it was enjoyed by the upper- and middle-class residents who lived in its vicinity.   —BDG

SKATING ON THE LADIES' SKATING-POND IN THE CENTRAL PARK, NEW YORK.

42. *Skating on the Ladies' Skating Pond in the Central Park, New York,* from *Harper's Weekly,* January 28, 1860, pp. 56–57

Wood engraving, 13⅞ x 20⅛ inches (35.3 x 51.8 cm). 1998.105.34, Gift of Harvey Isbitts

A chief factor in the rise of ice-skating's popularity was the opening to skaters of Central Park's lakes, which were reportedly first used by approximately three hundred people on a December Sunday in 1858. The fairly modest number ballooned to a staggering ten thousand by the following Sunday.[1] Activities on the various park ponds were strictly regulated. According to the unsigned article in the same *Harper's Weekly* issue that carried this illustration, the Gentlemen's Pond was

> *a large space, which, when the skating is good, may be seen covered with a couple of thousand people. Here every one may try his skill, and tumble about on the ice as he pleases. The Ladies' Pond is reserved for the fair sex, and no gentlemen are allowed to skate on it unless they are accompanied by ladies. It is kept in good order, and policemen on skates effectually repress all tendencies to rowdyism. . . . The scene when ladies are on the pond is attractive in the extreme, and*

> *usually draws a large concourse of visitors.* ("Skating on the Central Park," 58)

The strong reportorial nature and the topographical truthfulness of this image reflect Homer's aim to satisfy the intense public curiosity about Central Park, shown here in the first years of its use. The densely populated composition, filled with anecdotal motifs, links this panoramic view of the park and its society with Homer's earlier scenes of Boston. Here, as usual, Homer's dry wit sets the mood and is revealed especially in the man at the left foreground who shows off for the ladies, oblivious to the fact that he heads for thin ice. Perhaps, as was often the case, Homer intended this slice of narrative humor to carry a double meaning, for the sport of ice-skating was also widely known as a popular and (relatively) acceptable opportunity for flirtation, which, indeed, had its own pitfalls. —BDG

1. Roy Rosenzweig and Elizabeth Blackmar, *The Park and the People: A History of Central Park* (New York: Henry Holt and Company, 1992), 211.

HOMEWARD-BOUND.—[Drawn by Winslow Homer.]

43. *Homeward Bound,* from *Harper's Weekly,* December 21, 1867, pp. 808–9

Wood engraving, 13⅝ x 20½ inches (34.7 x 52.1 cm). 1998.105.101, Gift of Harvey Isbitts

Homer left for Europe in December 1866 and spent most of his approximately ten-month stay in Paris, where two of his paintings (*Prisoners from the Front* and *The Bright Side)* were shown in the Exposition Universelle. This engraving was doubtless inspired by Homer's own Atlantic crossing when he returned to the United States in the fall of 1867. Such ocean voyages allowed few creature comforts; walking on deck offered relief from the stale air of cramped cabins, although, as Homer shows, this activity was often achieved with difficulty. Choppy seas frequently caused the ship to roll to vertiginous angles, turning the daily stroll into a test of balance. Homer employed a bold compositional design to accentuate the sense of movement and instability. Not only does the deck itself tilt downward to the left, but it is also presented in a radical perspective that swiftly carries the eye toward a vanishing point at the distant end of the ship. The immediacy of the moment and the sensation that nothing is fixed are reinforced by the abrupt cropping of the two women seated in the foreground. Although it is tempting to attribute this unusually vigorous composition to Homer's absorption of trends he detected in avant-garde European art and to his liking for Japanese art as received through prints, there is no evidence to support or refute the supposition. It is just as likely that Homer, as an astute observer of his surroundings, responded to the confined but dramatic arena of shipboard life and chose to record it in the same dynamic way that he experienced it.　　　　—BDG

44. *Art Students and Copyists in the Louvre Gallery, Paris,*
from *Harper's Weekly,* January 11, 1868, p. 25

Wood engraving, 9 3/16 x 13 7/8 inches (23.4 x 35.2 cm). 1998.105.102, Gift of Harvey Isbitts

The *Harper's Weekly* issue in which this engraving appeared contained a brief history of the Louvre, which was introduced with a reference to Homer's illustration. Citing the engraving as "one of Mr. Winslow Homer's studies of Art-life in Paris, made during his late residence in the French capital," the piece then extolled the Louvre for its invaluable role in aiding aspiring artists in their studies ("The Louvre Gallery," 26). In this engraving, Homer concentrated on the growing number of women among the legions of art students training in Paris. These modern females are shown copying a monumental canvas of the Crucifixion or Deposition—an ambitious, time-honored subject—instead of the genteel floral still lifes and dainty watercolors that were considered "feminine" subjects and formats, and were normally associated with women's art production at that time. In essence, Homer addresses in this work the revolution in art education for women in the post–Civil War era. More specifically, this drawing provides solid evidence that Homer also visited the Louvre in the course of his own self-directed study during his ten-month stay in Europe in 1867, a period in his career that is only sparsely documented.   —BDG

WAITING FOR CALLS ON NEW-YEAR'S DAY.

45. *Waiting for Calls on New-Year's Day,* from *Harper's Bazar,* January 2, 1869, p. 9

Wood engraving, 9⅛ x 13¾ inches (23.3 x 35 cm). 1998.105.122, Gift of Harvey Isbitts

The custom of being "at home" to receive New Year's Day callers is featured in this engraving, which captures the varying moods of anticipation and boredom experienced by these elegantly attired urban women as they await their visitors. An 1870 article on the subject stated:

> The etiquette of New-Year's calls is very simple. The hospitalities of the day devolve entirely upon the ladies, who remain at home to receive any gentlemen friends that call to pay the compliments of the season. . . . [T]he hostess who is absent from the parlor when a guest enters commits a breach of New-Year's etiquette. She must be found there, and there she must remain, dispensing smiles and welcomes, surrounded by her daughters, if she have any, or by the bevy of ladies, the intimate friends, or the pretty cousins from the country, whom she has invited to receive with her.[1]

Although Homer's engraving surely illustrates the custom, the dejected aspect of the young woman seated in the center of the composition hints that a small domestic drama takes place. The girl is separate from her companions, not only because she is the only one seated, but also because she is physically unique among the group that is otherwise populated by fashion-plate types. What is more, her clothing is less elaborate and she rests in a simple wooden chair that does not match the other formal, upholstered furniture in the room. Such deliberate moves to differentiate the outward character of this one woman are indicative of the creative energy that Homer often invested in his commercial efforts, and they demonstrate one of the reasons why his illustrations are of such lasting interest.   —BDG

1. "New-Year's Calls," *Harper's Bazar,* January 1, 1870, 3.

SUMMER IN THE COUNTRY.

46. *Summer in the Country,*
from *Appletons' Journal of Literature, Science and Art,* July 10, 1869, p. 465

Wood engraving, 4½ x 6½ inches (11.6 x 16.7 cm). Engraved by John Karst. 1998.105.129, Gift of Harvey Isbitts

The game of croquet was imported to the United States from England in the early 1860s, and it soon became the most popular outdoor summer game in the country. As the text for *Summer in the Country* states, croquet was valued because it was a healthful "means of tempting young women into the air and sun." Moreover, young women (and men) also liked the game because it afforded a safe, socially acceptable opportunity for flirtation. It was noted elsewhere, "A correct eye, steady hands and nerves, good judgment and clear brain, are the essential qualifications for a good player, and the possession of these advantages, of course, is not dependent upon the age, sex or condition of the person."[1] For this engraving, Homer concentrated on strictly feminine society; the accompanying text offered the interpretation that these ladies came together out of "pure liking for the game, or love of out-of-doors" (465). Ironically, croquet's popularity diminished considerably shortly after Homer's engraving appeared because the game's health-promoting reputation was overshadowed by the politics of sexual innuendo that were attached to the game.[2]

—BDG

1. Prof. A. Rover, F. C. R. (pseud.), *Croquet: Its Principles and Rules, with Explanations and Illustrations for the lawn and parlor* (Springfield, Mass.: Milton Bradley and Co., 1877), 3, quoted in David Park Curry, *Winslow Homer: The Croquet Game,* exh. cat. (New Haven, Conn.: Yale University Art Gallery, 1984), unpag.

2. For Homer's depictions of the game and its subsequent decline, see Curry, *Winslow Homer: The Croquet Game.* Also see essay by Barbara Dayer Gallati in this volume.

WHAT SHALL WE DO NEXT?—[Drawn by Winslow Homer.]

47. *What Shall We Do Next?*, from *Harper's Bazar*, July 31, 1869, p. 488

Wood engraving, 9⅛ x 13¾ inches (23.3 x 35.3 cm). 1998.105.131, Gift of Harvey Isbitts

In this croquet subject, Homer explored the issue of modernity by contrasting country and city types. The distinction between the two modes of life is very clear in this composition, for the more sedate, conservative country girls remain on the porch either dutifully sewing or simply watching their fashionably dressed, more adventurous counterparts. The restlessness of the city girls is suggested by the caption for the picture—"What Shall We Do Next?"—while the restraint and discipline of country life are underscored by the plainly dressed young woman on the left who sits erect in her straight-back chair, ignoring the activities of the visitors from the city. By 1869 the national craze for croquet had taken firm hold. The game was promoted as a fine enticement for women to enter into physical exercise in the sunshine and open air, but its appeal on those grounds must have been considerably less compelling for residents of rural areas whose lifestyles already offered the same healthful benefits. —BDG

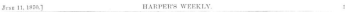

THE DINNER HORN.—[DRAWN BY WINSLOW HOMER.]

48. *The Dinner Horn,* from *Harper's Weekly,* June 11, 1870, p. 377

Wood engraving, 13⅞ x 9⅛ inches (35.4 x 23.3 cm). 1998.105.150, Gift of Harvey Isbitts

A young woman sounds the call for the noonday meal for the men laboring in the distant field. Gusts of wind pull her skirts behind her, investing her form with an almost heroic, monumental quality and offering a teasing glimpse of slim ankle. From 1870 to about 1873, Homer used a variation of this figure in several oil versions of this subject, all of which reflect his interest in depicting the wholesomeness of American farm life. The engraving provides greater narrative detail than the oils do, most likely indicating Homer's attentiveness to the demands of a general audience, which would anticipate and derive pleasure from such incidentals as the men in the field, the glimpse of the laid table through the doorway, or the cat that sinuously rubs itself on the jamb as it looks expectantly at the woman. The cat's response to the meal signal, perhaps a touch of Homer's own dry humor, parallels the field hands' ecstatic responses to the dinner horn, as if to suggest playfully the sirenlike power of the woman, vying with the powerful attraction of a home-cooked meal. A comparison of the illustration with oil versions of the image also reveals Homer's keen understanding of how to exploit the wood-engraving medium. In the engraving, he created additional visual interest in the pattern of the girl's dress, the border of spiked grasses at the lower edge of the composition, and the clean, light rectangular spot of ground from which the farm girl sounds the call.   —BDG

NEW SERIES, VOL. I, No. 34.]   SATURDAY, AUGUST 20, 1870.   [PRICE, 10 CENTS.

Entered according to Act of Congress, in the Year 1870, by Fields, Osgood, and Company, in the Clerk's Office of the District Court for the District of Massachusetts.

THE ROBIN'S NOTE. — BY WINSLOW HOMER. (SEE PAGE 531.)

49. *The Robin's Note,* from *Every Saturday,* August 20, 1870, cover

Wood engraving, 8⅞ x 9¼ inches (22.7 x 23.7 cm). 1998.105.155, Gift of Harvey Isbitts

Because this engraving did not accompany a literary text or topical news, Homer was able to engage a more personal style that approached that of his contemporaneous work in oils. Indeed, many of his paintings of the early 1870s feature young women in similar states of repose or reverie. His freedom from the demands of illustration is also strongly felt in the structure of the composition, in which simple, geometric shapes invigorate the pictorial space in a clear-cut pattern of lights and darks, and diagonal and vertical lines. A brief note of appreciation about the picture (which was the cover for this issue) appeared inside the magazine: "Our frontispiece of the week is a drawing from the pencil of Mr. Winslow Homer. The porch of a country house,—a hammock in the shade,—a pretty girl in the hammock,—a robin singing at intervals among the foliage,—these are the familiar objects out of which the artist has composed a charming summer picture, half picture and half poem. 'The Robin's Note' will, we think be endorsed by the reader." ("Illustrations. The Robin's Note," 531)   —BDG

50. *Cutting a Figure,* from *Every Saturday,* February 4, 1871, pp. 116–17

Wood engraving, 12⅞ x 19⅞ inches (32.8 x 50.6 cm). Engraved by W. H. Morse. 1998.105.167, Gift of Harvey Isbitts

The fashionable little coquette in this image functions as a charming seasonal "pinup." The viewer is invited to enjoy the wordplay, which calls for connecting the colloquial phrase "cutting a figure" (referring to the girl's stylishness) with her pursuit of literally cutting a figure in the ice. Rather than simply supplying a perfunctory illustration for a winter magazine issue, however, Homer created a fine picture that evokes the chill winter atmosphere and is filled with subtle compositional tensions (such as the relationship of the tree and its reflection in the ice that forms a rigid line along the length of the girl's body). Interestingly, the anonymously written comments directed to this double-page illustration valued it as a work of art:

> *Mr. Homer has not for a long time done any-thing more artistic than this drawing, which is no less careful in finish than design,*

reminding us of two or three paintings of his in the New York Academy of Design, a year or two since. The landscape portion of our engraving would be worthy of attention even without the figure, which occupies the foreground; but this figure is so thoroughly engaging with her sweet face and picturesque costume, that the spectator may be forgiven if he do not turn from her to observe how faithfully the artist has rendered the skating-ground, shut in by the leafless lines of trees, and the wintry sky beyond. (102)

—BDG

A COUNTRY STORE,—GETTING WEIGHED.

51. *A Country Store—Getting Weighed,* from *Every Saturday,* March 25, 1871, p. 272

Wood engraving, 9⅛ x 12 inches (23.3 x 30.5 cm). Engraved by William James Linton. 1998.105.168, Gift of Harvey Isbitts

Homer often contrasted the fashions and customs of the city with those of the country. Here urban and rural seem to blend in a group of well-dressed women in citified clothing looking on while a young woman is weighed by the country storekeeper. The store's plain, rustic interior acts as a finely detailed foil for the varied textures of the women's elaborate dresses and cloaks, and hints that they surely did not purchase their clothing locally. The engraving is exquisitely rendered and exemplifies the high-quality reproduction that could be attained in the aesthetic partnership between artist and master engraver.

A brief text appeared with the illustration, doubtless manufactured to fit Homer's work in this instance. After describing the country store in terms of its "maximum of miscellaneousness," the unidentified author referred to the engraving, creating a loose story line to satisfy the reader:

Pleasantly conspicuous among these [goods] are the pretty healthy girls who are indulging in the mild dissipation of being weighed. We may suppose that the gentleman who is dividing the avoirdupois among them is per-plexed to decide whether he shall tell the truth according to the scales and give them good weight, or shall flatter a sentimental weakness sometimes attributed to the sex by reporting them so light that they may regard themselves as quite ethereal creatures, angels with their wings just concealed. ("A Country Store—Getting Weighed," 271)

Homer also addressed the subject of the country store in an 1872 painting originally titled *A Rainy Day in the Country* (Hirshhorn Museum and Sculpture Garden, Smithsonian Institution), in which men converse as they warm themselves at an iron stove. That masculine version of the motif embodies the ultimate role of such a store in small communities where it functioned as the town's chief source of news and forum for casual political debate. Given Homer's tendency to conceive of content in terms of oppositions, it is possible that the engraving reveals his plans for a "feminine" counterpart painting that was never executed or has perhaps been lost.

—BDG

THE NOON RECESS.—Drawn by Winslow Homer.—[See Poem on Page 550.]

52. *The Noon Recess,* from *Harper's Weekly,* June 28, 1873, p. 549

Wood engraving, 9⅛ x 13⅝ inches (23.2 x 34.7 cm). 1998.105.174, Gift of Harvey Isbitts

Homer investigated the subject of the American country school in a series of oils, watercolors, and engravings beginning in the 1870s. His focus on the theme occurred at a crucial time of reform in American education, when teaching duties were taken over largely by women who were profession-ally trained, disciplinary tactics were modified, and new teaching methods reflected the rising belief in children's capacity to learn in a sympathetic environ-ment. *The Noon Recess* appeared opposite an anony-mously written poem of the same title that examined the emotional states of both figures:

Yes, hide your little tear-stained face
  Behind that well-thumbed book, my boy;
Your troubled thoughts are all intent
  Upon the game your mates enjoy,

While you this recess hour must spend
On study bench without a friend.

Ah, well! There's one grand lesson yet
  O'er which your tears must e'en be shed;
The problems of this changeful life
  Haye puzzled many a wiser head
Than yours may prove my little man;
So cling to sunshine while you can.

Ah! Weary one, whose brain is filled
  With tiresome sounds the livelong day,
E'en now your heart doth half incline
  To let the captive out to play;
For yonder some one waits for you:
  Shall love, or duty, find you true? (550)

—BDG

THE MORNING BELL.—Drawn by Winslow Homer.—[See Poem on Page 1114.]

53. *The Morning Bell,* from *Harper's Weekly,* December 13, 1873, p. 1116

Wood engraving, 9 ¼ x 13 ½ inches (23.7 x 34.5 cm). 1998.105.183, Gift of Harvey Isbitts

Homer's attentiveness to the growing industrialization of the nation is reflected in this engraving and his closely related 1871 oil originally titled *The Old Mill* (see the essay by Barbara Dayer Gallati, fig. 5). Unlike the painting, which features only a few women, the engraving includes a variety of workers as if to represent a cross section of the laboring community. Such differences notwithstanding, Homer's imagery remains focused on the women, as does the poem of the same title that acccompanied the engraving in *Harper's Weekly.* Indeed, Homer gave greater emphasis to the women on the right, here reducing their number to two, bringing them close to the picture plane, and modifying the pose of one so that she looks directly at the viewer. The physical contrasts displayed by these two key figures—one bent, tired, and resigned and the other alert and fresh—suggest the effects of an endless life of toil, a theme sounded in the poem:

> Not the late bell which rouses from sweet
>   dreams
>   Some Fair young sleeper in her downy
>   bed,
> And bids her rise to spend the new-born day
>   'Neath folly's rule, by fashion's sceptre led;

> Not the sweet bell which in the church
>   tower hangs
>   And calls with silvery tongue the hour of
>   prayer—
> Not that; for in response to its dear tones
>   The weary ones would find their rest from
>   care.

> Ah, no! 'tis but the heavy factory bell,
>   which takes its tone from factory noise
>   and din,
> And wearily responding to its call,
>   Behold the day of hardship must begin!

> And slowly in the well-worn, toilsome path
>   Go those whose paths seem ever cast in
>   shade,
> While others reap the sunshine of their toil:
>   By these the factory bell must be obeyed.

> And so the morning bell rings ever on,
>   And so the weary feet obey its call,
> Till o'er the earth silence at last shall come.
>   And death bring peace and rest alike to all.
> (1114)

—BDG

ON THE BEACH AT LONG BRANCH—THE CHILDREN'S HOUR.—[Drawn by Winslow Homer.]

54. *On the Beach at Long Branch—The Children's Hour,*
from *Harper's Weekly,* August 15, 1874, p. 672

Wood engraving, 9¼ x 13⅝ inches (23.7 x 34.7 cm). 1998.105.190, Gift of Harvey Isbitts

In this image Homer provides a glimpse of holiday life in terms of levels of society within the domestic sphere. The engraving was not accompanied by an explanatory text, but it suggests a narrative centering on a young woman (presumably the mother of the toddler and infant portrayed in the main figure group) who seems about to depart for the company of her social set, leaving her children in the charge of a nanny and a maid. Through careful observation of modes of dress, Homer not only made distinctions between leisure- and working-class women, but he also delineated the hierarchical differences between two members of household staff. Unlike his earlier works devoted to the pleasures of the shore (which include scantily clad bathers, flirtatious girls, and the mingling of the sexes), this engraving delivers a comparatively sober, conservative view of Long Branch, emphasizing the resort's propriety as a seasonal family residence. This message is most strongly felt in the dignified restraint of the central female, whose statuesque figure foreshadows the sturdy fisher girls of Homer's Cullercoats period of 1881–82.   —BDG

THE FAMILY RECORD.—Drawn by Winslow Homer, N.A.—[See Poem on Page 562.]

55. *The Family Record,* from *Harper's Bazar,* August 28, 1875, p. 561

Wood engraving, 13⅝ x 9⅛ (34.8 x 23.3 cm). 1998.105.131, Gift of Harvey Isbitts

Most of Homer's illustrations were intended to coincide with broad national sentiment. Themes of domestic harmony were particularly popular in the post–Civil War decades, when the unity of the family became a metaphor for the reunification of the country. *The Family Record* stresses the ideal of stability and continuity, as the young couple is observed inscribing the name of their infant in the family Bible under what may be presumed to be a portrait of a colonial ancestor. The engraving appeared on the page opposite the following anonymously published poem of the same title, quoted here in part:

> *"Ay, write it down in black and white—*
> *The date, the age, the name;*
> *For home has never seemed so dear*
> *As since our baby came.*
> *No child before was half so sweet,*
> *And never babe so wise;*
> *And, John, the neighbors say, indeed,*
> *It has its father's eyes."*
>
> . . . .

> *"For 'John' shall be his name, my dear.*
> *It is his father's own;*
> *And though a hundred more were given,*
> *I'll call him that alone.*
> *His father's eyes, his father's face,*
> *His father's form, I'm sure:*
> *God grant he have his father's heart,*
> *Life's hardships to endure!"*
>
> *"Well, there, 'tis written down at last;*
> *The record is complete.*
> *Henceforth we'll lay our loving hearts*
> *Beneath our baby's feet.*
> *Ah, wife, our home's a humble place—*
> *We're humble folks—that's true;*
> *But I'm a king with boundless wealth*
> *In that young rogue and you."* (562)

—BDG

RECREATION

Homer moved to New York City in the fall of 1859. Improvements in printing technology, the availability of paper, and a mass audience hungry for news and stories enriched with engraved images made the second half of the nineteenth century a golden age of American illustration, and New York City was the industry's center.

Although Homer is justly celebrated as an exceptional observer of the manners and mores of his period, these compelling images should not be read as literal records. In fact, the illustrations functioned as popular imagery does today, as subtle and convincing inventions reflecting and supporting mainstream taste and widely held ideas about social values, gender roles, and class relations. Even after Homer was established as one of the most famous of American illustrators and was able to exercise a degree of autonomy in assignment, his pictorial themes were still driven by the editorial policies of the magazines employing him and the prevailing tastes, interests, and concerns of an urban mass audience. Nevertheless, sharp observation, a sense of irony, and increasingly spare designs inform Homer's images with a subtle power that distinguishes them from more conventional work.

As Homer realized his ambitions to succeed as an academic artist during the 1860s and 1870s, subjects used in his oil paintings and watercolors also appeared in the popular press, spreading his reputation to a general audience as well as the elite patrons who frequented exhibitions. Nowhere do all of these issues emerge with more clarity than in Homer's images of American adults at play during the decade following the Civil War.   —LSF

OUR WATERING-PLACES—HORSE-RACING AT SARATOGA.—Drawn by Winslow Homer.—[See First Page.]

56. *Our Watering-Places—Horse-Racing at Saratoga,* from *Harper's Weekly,* August 26, 1865, p. 533

Wood engraving, 9 3/16 x 13 7/8 inches (23.3 x 35.2 cm). 1998.105.92, Gift of Harvey Isbitts

The term *watering place* was first used in the mid-eighteenth century to describe a resort visited by fashionable folk, either for sea bathing or for drinking or bathing in the waters of a mineral spring. Saratoga Springs, New York, was considered the premier summer resort for the social elite from the mid-1860s until the end of the nineteenth century. Then, as now, the town's tourist season reached its peak during August, when the historic track opened for racing. This event was reported in the article that this engraving illustrated: "Saratoga was all alive with excitement during the entire week beginning August 7. Every hotel and boarding-house and almost every private house was crowded. . . . The weather was as favorable as could have been desired, and the racing was without precedent" ("Horse-Racing at Saratoga," 529). Homer's image captures the excitement described by the article. Our point of view from the crowded grandstand high above the course plunges down upon the speeding horses below. The sharply tilted perspective reinforces the reckless excitement of the racing fever described above.　　　　—LSF

57. *Our National Winter Exercise—Skating,*
from *Frank Leslie's Illustrated Newspaper,* January 13, 1866, pp. 264–65

Wood engraving, 13⅞ x 20¼ inches (35.4 x 21.4 cm). 1998.105.96, Gift of Harvey Isbitts

Homer's artistic growth of the early 1860s can be observed by comparing his earlier skating subjects (for example, see pl. 42) with this image, in which the figure takes on a greater role in the overall compositional design. The physical grace and control required for skating are conveyed in the massing of the three figures dominating the left foreground—which together create a strong diagonal that bisects the composition. Their forms parallel each other, governing and unifying the rhythm of the composition. Such visual harmonies lend a stylish flair to the engraving, in which the eye is drawn from the dainty pointed feet of the two main skaters to the fluttering tips of their ribbons and veiling. These elegant young women contrast vividly with the less fortunate figure on the right, whose fall has left her sprawling, hoop skirt upturned and legs to the sky. Implicit in the scene are the commonly recognized opportunities for romance that were noted in the issue of the magazine: "The amount of matrimony and flirtation that will grow this year upon the ice will require many statisticians to keep count of, and the amount of real fun outside of that can never be kept count of" ("Skating," 263).

Just as Homer's art was maturing, so too, was the status of ice-skating. The sport had initially grabbed the nation's attention in the late 1850s and, by 1866, was so popular that the writer of the text accompanying this illustration could state confidently that "the papers chronicle the daily condition of Central park pond, the 5th Avenue pond, and all the other ponds, with as much avidity as they once chronicled 'the war.'"

—BDG

THE ARTIST IN THE COUNTRY. By Winslow Homer.

58. *The Artist in the Country,*
from *Appletons' Journal of Literature, Science and Art,* June 19, 1869, cover

Wood engraving, 6¼ x 6⁹⁄₁₆ inches (15.8 x 16.1 cm). Engraved by John Karst. 1998.160.13. Gift of Harvey Isbitts

This amusing vignette documents Homer's own activity as a *plein-air* painter. Although the figure is portrayed from behind, the porkpie hat and mustache clearly resemble Homer's own. Intent upon his canvas of a wilderness subject, the artist in the illustration sits on a camp stool at a portable easel under a white umbrella. A knapsack in the right foreground is evidence of the overland trek required to reach such a remote site. Nevertheless, the popularity of the White Mountain wilderness (see p. 108) as a tourist destination is also indicated by the presence of a well-dressed young lady who, like the reader, watches the artist at work. A choice of narratives is offered by the text:

As to the painter's companion in Mr. Winslow Homer's sketch, we will let our readers frame what romance pertaining to her they may please. A love-story could be woven out of the situation, although some crusty critic might declare that the man is far too much absorbed in his labors, too utterly heedless of the young woman at his elbow, for their relationship to be any thing [sic] else but that of man and wife. But let each of our readers decide this for himself. ("Table-Talk," 378)

—LSF

THE SUMMIT OF MOUNT WASHINGTON.—Drawn by Winslow Homer.—[See Page 446.]

59. *The Summit of Mount Washington,* from *Harper's Weekly,* July 10, 1869, p. 441

Wood engraving, 9 x 13¾ inches (22.8 x 35 cm). 1998.160.14, Gift of Harvey Isbitts

Spreading across northern New Hampshire and into Maine is the most mountainous region in New England—named the White Mountains for the blanket of snow that covers the area during much of the year. By the 1860s the White Mountains were as popular a summer destination as the Catskills. Homer first traveled to the region in 1868, finding subjects for magazine illustrations as well as oil paintings. This vivid image records the last stages of the ascent at a height indicated by the cloud banks wafting by. The party in the foreground ascends on horseback, while more hardy hikers make their way on foot to the distant lodge glimpsed in the upper left. The text described the vista:

Mount Washington is the highest mountain in New England, rising 6285 feet above the level of the sea. . . . Our illustration . . . represents the summit of this peak, and is a picturesque representation of the scene which it portrays. As one ascends the mountain vegetation gradually disappears. Soon only dwarf pines are visible; at length even these disappear, and the only indication of vegetable life is the lichen; upon the top of the mountain the rocks lay absolutely naked to the sky, as shown in our picture. ("The Summit of Mount Washington," 446)

—LSF

THE STRAW RIDE.—[See Page 619.]

60. *The Straw Ride*, from *Harper's Bazar*, September 25, 1869, p. 620

Wood engraving, 9³⁄₁₆ x 13⅞ inches (23.3 x 35.2 cm). 1998.105.136, Gift of Harvey Isbitts

Excursions in old-fashioned vehicles like farm wag-ons gained in nostalgic charm as rapid transit by rail-road replaced earlier forms of transportation. Holiday recreation in the countryside was extolled not only for its health benefits but also for the oppor-tunities it provided for greater social latitude, cele-brated here in the informal proximity of young men and women. An ironic reference is also made in the accompanying text to waning distinctions between "city folks" and their "country cousins" through fashion information provided by widely read period-icals such as *Harper's Bazar:*

> That peculiarly American institution, the Straw Ride, which our artist has so well

depicted, will be familiar to our readers who know any thing of New England country life. . . . It is needless to describe the fun and jollity that accompany these rides, which are appreciated by city folks as well as their country cousins, to judge from the illustra-tion—unless, indeed, the latter have so far profited by the wise counsels of the Bazar that they are no longer distinguishable by the cut of their clothes. ("The Straw Ride," 619)

—LSF

61. *The Fishing Party,*
from *Appletons' Journal of Literature, Science and Art,* October 2, 1869, supplement

Wood engraving, 9 x 12 ¼ inches (22.9 x 32.3 cm). Engraved by John Filmer. 1998.105.138, Gift of Harvey Isbitts

Fishing was one of the sports newly available to women as a "refined diversion" after the Civil War. The convenience of lightweight equipment and a higher degree of social freedom encouraged "the piscatorial efforts of the ladies."[1] Nevertheless, the tone of humorous condescension expressed in the text accompanying Homer's illustration suggests certain limits to female participation in what was still a traditionally male pursuit:

> *Among the various things that women cannot do as well as men, Miss [Susan B.] Anthony to the contrary notwithstanding, are whist-playing and angling.... Ladies possess one qualification for such a pursuit,*

and that is patience. But, as they must chatter, and get easily excited, and as a class utterly lack that precision so necessary for the art, angling is always a little too much for them.... But all this does not prevent Mr. Homer's picture from affording us many delightful suggestions, and ... who would not like to wander, in just such company, along the picturesque banks of the Sawkill. ("Table Talk," 218)

—LSF

1. David Tatham, *Winslow Homer in the Adirondacks* (Syracuse, N.Y.: Syracuse University Press, 1996), 57–58.

UNDER THE FALLS, CATSKILL MOUNTAINS.—[FROM A PAINTING BY WINSLOW HOMER.]

62. *Under the Falls, Catskill Mountains*, from *Harper's Weekly*, September 14, 1872, p. 721

Wood engraving, 9¼ x 13⅞ inches (23.7 x 35.4 cm). 1998.105.172, Gift of Harvey Isbitts

Homer's first visit to the Catskill region in 1871 was the occasion for an excursion to Kaaterskill Falls that he recorded in this view. These dramatic waterfalls in the Catskill Clove are still a landmark, not far from where the famous hotel popularly known as the Catskill Mountain House stood from 1824 until it was demolished in 1963. Homer depicted the cave behind the falls, once celebrated by Thomas Cole and others as a forbidding and solitary place, but by this time thoroughly domesticated by the presence of fashionable tourists. *Picturesque America*, an elaborately illustrated two-volume text on the scenic beauty of the United States published in 1874,

described the visitor's experience from the hiking trail seen in Homer's image: "Standing on the narrow pathway, you look through the great white veil of falling waters, leaping out over your head and sending up clouds of spray that float off down the gorge. Sometimes, when the sun is shining brightly, a dancing rainbow will keep pace with you as you creep around the semicircle beneath the rock."[1]   —LSF

1. William Cullen Bryant, ed., *Picturesque America; or, The Land We Live In* (New York: D. Appleton & Company, 1874), vol. 2, p. 126.

FLIRTING ON THE SEA-SHORE AND ON THE MEADOW.—[DRAWN BY WINSLOW HOMER.]

63. *Flirting on the Sea-Shore and on the Meadow,*
from *Harper's Weekly,* September 19, 1874, p. 780

Wood engraving, 9¼ x 13⅝ inches (23.5 x 34.8 cm). 1998.105.194, Gift of Harvey Isbitts

Homer's double register of witty illustrations needed no text to remind the reader that another popular summer recreation was the game of playing at courtship known as flirting. His images offer a set of variations on the theme, contrasting the beach and countryside; moonlight and high noon; and the worlds of adults and children. The dark pyramid formed by the couple near the waves reinforces a sense of secret assignation and erotic mystery. Broad daylight, in contrast, illuminates the encounter of two prone farm boys rapt in their mutual admiration of the little girl who sits before them. The humor of children playing at such courtship is suggested by the family of ducks marching into the left foreground— a visual play on the ultimate outcome of such courting rituals.   —LSF

THE COASTAL RESORT

A recurrent theme in Homer's illustrations during the late 1860s and early 1870s was the summertime activity at coastal resorts and fashionable watering places including the North and South Shore near Boston; Newport, Rhode Island; and the most recently developed seaside destination, Long Branch, New Jersey. On holiday excursions, social controls were relaxed as men and women in bathing costumes cavorted together in the water. Reactions to this activity ranged from ambivalence that it was "not quite refined" to outrage and ridicule. The erotic attraction of young women in bathing suits was frequently remarked upon. *Harper's Weekly* commented on such sights in 1873: "During bathing hours, at this season of the year, the beaches at all our fashionable sea-side resorts present the most animated and, it must be confessed, most grotesque spectacle."[1] All of these motifs, as well as the more restrained social rituals of the coastal resorts, offered rich pictorial opportunities for Homer, who followed the crowds on their summer treks to Long Branch and other fashionable seaside destinations. A number of such modern-life subjects also found their way into his oil paintings.   —LSF

---

1. "Sea-Bathers," *Harper's Weekly,* August 2, 1873, 671.

HARPER'S WEEKLY. [AUGUST 27, 1859.] 553

AUGUST IN THE COUNTRY—THE SEA-SHORE.

64. *August in the Country—The Sea-Shore,* from *Harper's Weekly,* August 27, 1859, p. 553

Wood engraving, 9⅛ x 13¾ inches (23.3 x 35 cm). 1998.105.27, Gift of Harvey Isbitts

"The scene by the sea-side—the *dolce far niente*—the hunt for *crustacea*—the hour spent in sketching the distant schooner—the delightful *tetes-a-tete*—are they not all written in our memories?" ("August in Town and at the Sea-Side," 554). Accompanied by such nostalgic musings, this illustration is one of Homer's earliest images of seaside recreation. The busy composition, filled with figural anecdotes drawn from the conventions of humorous genre painting and caricature, offers a marked contrast to the more sophisticated representation of seaside episodes in the designs that the artist created a decade later.   —LSF

65. *Art Supplement to Appletons' Journal—The Beach at Long Branch,*
from *Appletons' Journal of Literature, Science and Art,* August 21, 1869, p. 624

Wood engraving, 13 x 19½ inches (33 x 49.6 cm). Engraved by John Karst. 1998.105.134, Gift of Harvey Isbitts

Life at the seaside provided the subject for an elaborate two-page illustration, or "art supplement," and its accompanying text:

> *Mr. Winslow Homer . . . gives us a picture of the ease and pleasurable abandon which accompany life at Long Branch. On the beach, more than anywhere else in the world, society throws aside its dignity. Men and women make children of themselves. Those in the water give themselves up to sport, frolicking with each other and with the waves, thoughtless of fashion and its formalities. . . . Our artist suggests an old poetic thought in the letters drawn, by a young girl, in the sand. Something of tenderness, which she would hardly acknowledge, perhaps, has guided her hand; her friend may study her thoughts by the point of her umbrella; the next tide will efface the letters forever; let us hope that the artist means no reflection on the fidelity of the sex. The shallow film of water, which washes away so many letters in the sand, is a very suggestive symbol of coquetry. Many a name, however, has been written "on the beach at Long Branch," which has never been effaced—the beach has gladdened more hearts than it has saddened, despite its reputation—it has made more matches than it has broken.* ("On the Beach at Long Branch," 23)

HIGH TIDE. — From a Painting by Winslow Homer. (See Page 499.)

66. *High Tide,* from *Every Saturday,* August 6, 1870, p. 504

Wood engraving, 9¼ x 12⅛ inches (23.6 x 31 cm). 1998.105.152, Gift of Harvey Isbitts

"Sea-bathing," as it was called, was an activity to be approached with caution at this time. A contemporary article advised: "[T]he question, to bathe or not to bathe in public, will always remain an open one. By taking proper precautions one can be pretty sure of not outraging the proprieties, but of not making himself a ridiculous object,—a spectacle to be derided and howled at,—who can be sure?"[1] The trio of young women shown here may reflect such ambivalence in their curious estrangement from each other and sober attitudes as they emerge from the waves on an empty beach. This engraving was based on a painting by Homer exhibited at the National Academy of Design in 1870 as *Manners and Customs at the Seashore.* Although popular illustrations often exploited the titillating aspects of lightly clad females on the beach, Homer's subject was a daring one for an oil painting.

—LSF

1. "Long Branch: The American Boulogne," *Every Saturday,* August 26, 1871, 214.

67. *Low Tide*, from *Every Saturday*, August 6, 1870, p. 505

Wood engraving, 9¼ x 12⅛ inches (23.5 x 30.8 cm). Engraved by W. H. Kingdon. 1998.105.153, Gift of Harvey Isbitts

Both *High Tide* and *Low Tide*, published in Boston's short-lived weekly *Every Saturday* in August 1870, are illustrations after Homer's oil paintings. *High Tide* is now known as *Eagle Head, Manchester, Massachusetts*, 1870 (The Metropolitan Museum of Art, New York). Disheartened by the critical recep-tion of these works, Homer apparently destroyed the painting of *Low Tide*. When the owner of *High Tide* approached Homer to buy the companion painting, he was told that the picture had been painted out and the canvas reused for another work.   —LSF

ON THE BLUFF AT LONG BRANCH, AT THE BATHING HOUR.—[Drawn by Winslow Homer.]

68. *On the Bluff at Long Branch, at the Bathing Hour,* from *Harper's Weekly,* August 6, 1870, p. 504

Wood engraving, 9 x 13 inches (23 x 35 cm). 1998.105.154, Gift of Harvey Isbitts

After the Civil War, Long Branch, New Jersey, became one of the leading playgrounds of the Atlantic seaboard, attracting visitors from the fashionable and theatrical world, although it never enjoyed the exclusivity of Newport or Saratoga. An 1869 article in *Appletons' Journal of Literature, Science and Art* noted: "Long Branch is . . . cosmopolitan . . . because it fairly represents the city of New York. . . . Like New York, it is an epitome of the entire country. Cape May belongs to Philadelphia, and is in no sense cosmopolitan. Newport is now a city of cottages, and is to be compared no longer with those summer resorts which are sought by the transient public. Nahant is the midsummer synonyme of Boston. Long Branch is the representative 'sea-shore' of the nation."[1] In Homer's vivid image, a bevy of windblown, fashionable ingenues, drawn by the white flag announcing calm water, approaches the steep wooden staircase that led from the top of the high sand dunes known as the Bluff to the bathhouses on the wide beach below. Many of these pictorial motifs also appear in one of Homer's most famous oil paintings, *The Beach at Long Branch*, 1869 (Museum of Fine Arts, Boston).   —LSF

1. "On the Beach at Long Branch," *Appletons' Journal of Literature, Science and Art,* August 21, 1869, 23.

ON THE BEACH AT LONG BRANCH.

69. *On the Beach at Long Branch,* from *Harper's Bazar,* September 3, 1870, p. 569

Wood engraving, 8 15/16 x 13 3/4 inches (22.7 x 35 cm). 1998.105.156, Gift of Harvey Isbitts

Driving in an open coach was a popular leisure activity at seaside resorts. Such drives were a daily form of social ritual, displaying both the carriage and its occupants. Homer's radically cropped composition reduces the coach (and the liveried male driver) to a framework for a trio of well-dressed beauties. The artist's emphasis on details of their dress, coiffure, and accessories approaches the conventional fashion plate in this illustration, which has no accompanying text. Nevertheless, Homer captures our imagination and suggests a narrative with the elaborate costumes and lively conversation taking place among these young women, oblivious to the ocean view beyond.

—LSF

70. Bathing at Long Branch, — *"Oh, Ain't It Cold!"*
from *Every Saturday,* August 26, 1871, p. 213

Wood engraving, 9⅛ x 12⅛ inches (23.3 x 31 cm). Engraved by W. H. Morse. 1998.105.170, Gift of Harvey Isbitts

This full-page image accompanied a lengthy article on "Long Branch: The American Boulogne," comparing the New Jersey resort to a famous French watering place. Homer selected the following episode to illustrate, mindful no doubt of the appeal of young girls in bathing suits:

> By this time it is past ten o'clock; the white flag which signals the fashionable moments of ablution has been fluttering for a half-hour, and a stream of bathers begins to set toward the beach. . . . [T]hree young girls . . . are now running gayly together . . . their slender figures . . . clad in perfectly fitting garments of bright colored flannel, and their dark brown hair bewitchingly tucked up under dainty oil-skin caps. A simultaneous rush and a plunge, and in an instant the triad have risen all dripping and breathless, and their peculiar cringing posture and the shrinking motion of the arms across the bosom, even without the stirring of their lips, suggest the familiar words "Oh! Isn't it cold?" (214)

—LSF

THE BATHERS.—FROM A PICTURE BY WINSLOW HOMER.—[SEE PAGE 671.]

71. *The Bathers,* from *Harper's Weekly,* August 2, 1873, p. 668

Wood engraving, 13⅞ x 9¼ inches (35.4 x 23.7 cm). Engraved by William H. Redding. 1998.105.175, Gift of Harvey Isbitts

This illustration was accompanied by a comment on the vicissitudes of bathing costumes:

> *Nothing could be prettier or more bewitching than the sight of a charming young woman in an elegant and tasteful bathing costume, as she trips over the sand from the dressing-house down to the water's edge. . . . But coming out! According to the old fable Venus sprang from the sea, but she was encumbered with no other bathing costume than her own luxuriant and flowing locks. . . . Can it be that this dripping, bedraggled, forlorn object who comes slowly from the water is the nymph-like creature who excited such admiration a few minutes ago? What a laughable disillusion! . . . The pretty figures in the foreground of Mr. Winslow Homer's charming picture . . . are perhaps an exception to the general rule, and illustrate the advantages of a costume peculiarly adapted to a graceful exit from the bath.* ("Sea-Bathers," 671)

THE WRECK OF THE "ATLANTIC"—CAST UP BY THE SEA.—DRAWN BY WINSLOW HOMER.—[SEE PAGE 342.]

72. *The Wreck of the "Atlantic"—Cast Up by the Sea,* from *Harper's Weekly,* April 26, 1873, p. 345

Wood engraving, 9⅛ x 13⅞ inches (23.3 x 35.4 cm). 1998.105.173, Gift of Harvey Isbitts

The ocean coast had its dangers as well as its attractions. Shipwreck was a pervasive fear in the nineteenth century. Maritime disasters like the loss of the *Atlantic* off the coast of Newfoundland were regularly reported in the newspapers and magazines. Homer's image, at once pathetic and erotic, of "one of the many painful incidents of the days following the breaking up of the wreck" (342), is based not only on actual reports of the *Atlantic* tragedy, but also, it has been suggested, on an earlier literary source, Henry Wadsworth Longfellow's *The Wreck of the Hesperus* (1839).[1] That famous ballad closed with a grisly discovery: "At daybreak, on the bleak sea-beach, / A fisherman stood aghast, / To see the form of a maiden fair, / Lashed close to a drifting mast. / The salt sea was frozen on her breast, / The salt tears in her eyes; / And he saw her hair, like the brown sea-weed; / On the billows fall and rise."[2]   —LSF

1. Philip C. Beam, *Winslow Homer's Magazine Engravings* (New York: Harper & Row, 1979), 23.
2. *Poems by Henry Wadsworth Longfellow* (Philadelphia: Henry C. Baird, 1850), 53–54.

THE COUNTRYSIDE AND THE ADIRONDACKS

Homer's attachment to country life found expression in his illustrations and paintings during the 1870s. His regular visits to Houghton Farm near Mountainville, New York, the summer retreat of family friends, provided the subjects and setting for many works. Rural pastimes, often featuring children, provided a counterpart to the more urbane amusements depicted in Homer's illustrations of fashionable summer resorts. His images also reflect the seasonal cycles of country life and farming. In Homer's time, such celebrations of the rural world were exercises in nostalgia as the United States evolved from an agrarian to an industrial economy.

Homer also traveled to more remote regions of New York, exploring the Adirondack Wilderness, located in the North Country. After the Civil War, sportsmen came there to hunt and fish and were joined by increasing numbers of tourists and artists eager for a "wilderness" experience. Homer, an ardent outdoorsman and fisherman, first visited the region in 1870 and returned regularly over the course of his career. His destination was a farm at Baker's Clearing (later a private preserve known as the North Woods Club) located near Minerva, New York, and the site of excellent fishing. These excursions provided the subjects for some of Homer's most famous oils and watercolors, as well as for images that appeared in the illustrated press during the 1870s.

—LSF

SPRING FARM WORK—GRAFTING.—[FROM A DRAWING BY WINSLOW HOMER.]

73. *Spring Farm Work—Grafting,* from *Harper's Weekly,* April 30, 1870, p. 276

Wood engraving, 7 x 9⅛ inches (18 x 23.3 cm). 1998.105.148, Gift of Harvey Isbitts

A solitary country youth is framed high in the still-bare branches of a fruit tree in spring. With shirt-sleeves rolled up and balanced on a ladder with a basket of tools and twigs suspended nearby, he is intent on inserting shoots, or grafts, into slits in the branches that he has pruned. Grafting, a method of improving the stock of fruit trees, here embodies the human control over nature of good husbandry.

Below, we see a farmyard with neatly stacked hay mounds and tidy outbuildings, reinforcing the sense of a well-regulated precinct of agricultural industry. Accurate but idealized images of land under cultivation like this one operated as metaphors for social harmony and good governance and were often set up as contrasts to and critiques of modern life in the city.

—LSF

SPRING BLOSSOMS.—[Drawn by Winslow Homer.]

74. *Spring Blossoms,* from *Harper's Weekly,* May 21, 1870, p. 328

Wood engraving, 9¼ x 13⅞ inches (23.6 x 35.4 cm). 1998.105.149, Gift of Harvey Isbitts

This illustration recorded another step in the seasonal cycle of good agricultural management and contrasted labor with leisure. A group of happy city and country dwellers enjoys the benefits of the solitary grafter's skills in the spectacular blooming tree that now arches protectively above them (and which will later bear further bounty in the form of fruit). The combination of blooms and fragrance induces spring fever; adults meditate in a dreamy state while the children lounge about. Homer participates in this idyllic scene by playfully emblazoning his initials on the sail of a toy boat plying the waters in the trough.

—LSF

A WINTER-MORNING, · SHOVELLING OUT. — DRAWN BY WINSLOW HOMER.   (SEE PAGE 30.)

75. *A Winter-Morning, Shovelling Out,* from *Every Saturday,* January 14, 1871, p. 32

Wood engraving, 9 ¼ x 12 ⅛ inches (23.6 x 31 cm). Engraved by G. A. Avery. 1998.105.164, Gift of Harvey Isbitts

One of the most felicitous passages in Mr. Whittier's exquisite Winter Idyl, "Snow-Bound," is that in which he describes the heavy snow-fall that buried everything but the trees and shut up the dwellers in a country house more securely than a sheriff can. The blood of the youngsters leaped to their finger ends when they heard their father's laconic order: "Boys, a path!" On page 32 Mr. Winslow Homer sketches a similar scene. The boys are digging out to the street, throwing the large light blocks of snow right and left, while one of the sisters, with a tenderness that does honor to her sex, is feeding the birds whose breakfast elsewhere is fatally beyond scratching distance. Our readers who have been in the country during or just after a heavy snow-storm will appreciate the fidelity and power with which Mr. Homer has represented the scene.

(From the text published with the engraving, "A Winter Morning,—Shovelling Out," 30)

TRAPPING IN THE ADIRONDACKS. — DRAWN BY WINSLOW HOMER. (SEE PAGE 838.)

76. *Trapping in the Adirondacks,* from *Every Saturday,* December 24, 1870, p. 849

Wood engraving, 9 ¼ x 12 ⅛ inches (23.7 x 31 cm). Engraved by John Parker Davis. 1998.105.158, Gift of Harvey Isbitts

The illustration needs no key. The sportsman has just drawn from the water a fine specimen of Adirondack game, and seems to be contemplating it with severe composure. The scenery will be recognized by visitors to the Wilderness, as a faithful representation of Adirondack woods and waters. ("Trapping in the Adirondacks," 838)

Once again Homer departed from convention (and the accompanying text) to depict a pair of guides and hands from Baker's Clearing. While traditional sporting images focused on the elite visitors, or "sportsmen," David Tatham notes that Homer chose the local labor force to serve as his subjects. Here he depicted Charles Lancaster and Rufus Wallace checking traps on Mink Pond in late summer or early fall.[1] The distinctive profile of Beaver Mountain rises at the right. These Adirondack landmarks and regional types would appear again and again in Homer's paintings and watercolors in the coming decades.

—LSF

1. David Tatham, *Winslow Homer in the Adirondacks* (Syracuse, N.Y.: Syracuse University Press, 1996), 38–39.

77. Deer-Stalking in the Adirondacks in Winter, from *Every Saturday*, January 21, 1871, p. 57

Wood engraving, 9⅛ x 12 inches (23.3 x 30.6 cm). 1998.105.165, Gift of Harvey Isbitts

Mr. Winslow Homer presents an effective sketch of one aspect of winter sporting in the Adirondack Wilderness. When the snow is so deep as to hinder the deer, the sportsmen put on snow-shoes, which . . . are . . . helpful in keeping the hunter out of the snow and enabling him to traverse the wilderness on its surface with a rapidity and noiselessness which are fatal to the deer. The readers of Every Saturday who feel the Nimrod instinct strong within them will appreciate the salient features of Mr. Homer's picture, and almost hear the baying of the deep-mouthed hounds as they overtake the game. ("Deer-Stalking in the Adirondacks," 54)

The narratives accompanying Homer's Adirondack illustrations assumed that the figures in these scenes were outsiders to the region known as sportsmen— primarily urban males drawn by the opportunities to hunt and fish. David Tatham has nevertheless identified most of these figures by feature and dress as local residents whom the artist knew from his visits to Baker's Clearing. During the hunting season, these woodsmen acted as guides and hands to the visitors. They, themselves, hunted for subsistence rather than sport.[1]

—LSF

---

1. David Tatham, *Winslow Homer in the Adirondacks* (Syracuse, N.Y.: Syracuse University Press, 1996), 41.

78. *Lumbering in Winter,* from *Every Saturday,* January 28, 1871, p. 89

Wood engraving, 12⅛ x 9⅛ inches (30.9 x 23.4 cm). Engraved by John Parker Davis. 1998.105.166, Gift of Harvey Isbitts

Our artist presents an effective picture of lumbermen engaged in their winter work. The scene represents the first stage of lumbering,—felling trees and cutting them into logs of the desired length. In Maine, in the Adirondacks, in Michigan, and about the upper waters of the Mississippi, as well as on the Pacific coast, this work is always done in winter,—large gangs of men striking out into the vast forests, where they spend the season in getting timber ready to be floated to the innumerable sawmills which vex the main watercourses sometimes hundreds of miles below. ("Lumbering in Winter," 78)

While the narrative accompanying this illustration discusses the image in the context of the commercial lumber industry, David Tatham has suggested that Homer actually depicted "farm cutting," or the felling of trees on the Baker family's land for their own use. The artist has telescoped two events— felling a tree and splitting logs—into dangerously close proximity.[1]

—LSF

1. David Tatham, *Winslow Homer in the Adirondacks* (Syracuse, N.Y.: Syracuse University Press, 1996), 41.

CAMPING OUT IN THE ADIRONDACK MOUNTAINS.—[DRAWN BY WINSLOW HOMER.]

79. *Camping Out in the Adirondack Mountains,*
from *Harper's Weekly,* November 7, 1874, p. 920

Wood engraving, 9⅛ x 13¾ inches (23.3 x 35 cm). Engraved by W. H. Lagarde. 1998.105.195, Gift of Harvey Isbitts

In the last Adirondack image that Homer prepared for the illustrated press, he once again presented local woodsmen in a familiar and favorite setting. Rufus Wallace and a companion sit before a bark lean-to on the shore of Mink Pond before a smudge fire burning to keep away insects.[1] The nearby canoe, assorted fishing paraphernalia, and a string of fish announce the end of a successful day on the pond. An enthusiastic fisherman, Homer may well have participated in this excursion as both angler and artist.   —LSF

---

1. David Tatham, *Winslow Homer in the Adirondacks* (Syracuse, N.Y.: Syracuse University Press, 1996), 59.

Beam, Philip C. *Winslow Homer's Magazine Engravings.* New York: Harper & Row, Publishers, 1979.

Benjamin, S. G. W. *Our American Artists.* Second series. Boston: D. Lothrop & Co., 1881. Reprint, edited and with an introduction by H. Barbara Weinberg, New York: Garland Publishing, 1977.

Bradley, W. A. "Modern American Wood-Engraving." Article from unidentified periodical, paginated 609–13. Art Reference Library, Brooklyn Museum of Art.

Burns, Sarah. "Barefoot Boys and Other Country Children: Sentiment and Ideology in Nineteenth-Century American Art." *American Art Journal* 20 (1988): 24–50.

———. *Pastoral Inventions: Rural Life in Nineteenth-Century American Art and Culture.* Philadelphia: Temple University Press, 1989.

Cikovsky, Nicolai, Jr. "Winslow Homer's *School Time.*" In *In Honor of Paul Mellon, Collector and Benefactor,* ed. John Wilmerding, 47–69. Washington, D.C.: National Gallery of Art, 1986.

———. "Winslow Homer's (So-Called) *Morning Bell.*" *American Art Journal* 29 (1998): 4–17.

Cikovsky, Nicolai, Jr., and Franklin Kelly. *Winslow Homer.* Exh. cat. Washington, D.C., New Haven, Connecticut: National Gallery of Art and Yale University Press, 1995.

Cole, Timothy. "Some Difficulties of Wood-Engraving." *Print-Collector's Quarterly* 1 (July 1911): 335–43.

Cooper, Helen. *Winslow Homer Watercolors.* Exh. cat. Washington, D.C., New Haven, Connecticut: National Gallery of Art and Yale University Press, 1986.

Cornell Fine Arts Museum, Rollins College. *Winslow Homer the Illustrator: His Wood Engravings 1857–1888.* Exh. cat. Winter Park, Florida: Rollins College, 1990.

Cowdrey, Mary Bartlett. *Winslow Homer: Illustrator.* Exh. cat. Northampton, Massachusetts: Smith College Museum of Art, 1951.

Cundall, Joseph. *A Brief History of Wood-Engraving, from Its Invention.* London: Sampson Low, Marston, and Company, 1895.

Curry, David Park. *Winslow Homer: The Croquet Game.* Exh. cat. New Haven, Connecticut: Yale University Art Gallery, 1984.

"Fine Art." *Nation,* February 4, 1875, 84.

Foster, Allen Evarts. *A Check List of Illustrations by Winslow Homer in* Harper's Weekly *and Other Periodicals.* New York: The New York Public Library, 1936.

———. "A Check List of Illustrations by Winslow Homer Appearing in Various Periodicals." *Bulletin of The New York Public Library* 44 (July 1940): 537–39.

Foster, Kathleen. "Makers of the American Watercolor Movement: 1860–1890." Ph.D. dissertation, Yale University, New Haven, Connecticut, 1982.

Gelman, Barbara, ed. *The Wood Engravings of Winslow Homer.* New York: Bounty Books, A Division of Crown Publishers, 1969.

Goodrich, Lloyd. *Winslow Homer.* New York: The Macmillan Company, 1944.

———. *The Graphic Art of Winslow Homer.* New York: The Museum of Graphic Art, 1968.

———. *Winslow Homer in Monochrome.* New York: M. Knoedler & Co., 1987.

———. Papers. City University of New York, Lloyd Goodrich and Edith Havens Goodrich, Whitney Museum of American Art, Record of the Works of Winslow Homer.

Hamilton, Sinclair. *Early American Book Illustrators and Wood Engravers 1670–1870.* Princeton, New Jersey: Princeton University Library, 1958.

Jussim, Estelle. *Visual Communication and the Graphic Arts.* New York: R. R. Bowker Company, 1974.

Kelly, James Edward. Papers. Archives of American Art, Smithsonian Institution, Washington, D.C.

Kelsey, Mavis Parrott. *Winslow Homer Graphics.* Houston: The Museum of Fine Arts, 1977.

Kingsley, Elbridge. "Life and Works of Elbridge Kingsley Painter-Engraver Consisting of Paintings in Oil and Water Colors, Photographs from Paintings reproduced in Engraving, Japan proofs & Plain Prints Experiments with Process Plate." Undated typescript. Archives of American Art, Smithsonian Institution, Washington, D.C.

Linton, W. J. *The History of Wood-Engraving in America.* Boston: Estes and Sauriat, 1881.

Mather, Frank Jewett, Jr. "Winslow Homer as a Book Illustrator." *Princeton University Library Chronicle* 11, no. 1 (1939): 15–32.

Mott, Frank Luther. *History of American Magazines 1850–1865.* Cambridge, Massachusetts: Harvard University Press, 1938.

The New York Public Library Clipping Files: James Langridge, John Filmer, Edward Sears, J. P. Davis, William James Linton.

O'Gorman, James F. *This Other Gloucester: Occasional Papers on the Arts of Cape Ann Massachusetts.* Gloucester, Massachusetts: Ten Pound Island Book Company, 1990.

Simpson, Marc, et al. *Winslow Homer: Paintings of the Civil War.* Exh. cat. San Francisco: The Fine Arts Museums of San Francisco and Bedford Arts, Publishers, 1988.

Spassky, Natalie. *Winslow Homer.* Exh. brochure. New York: The Metropolitan Museum of Art, 1979.

Stanton, Joseph. "Winslow Homer, Helena de Kay and Richard Watson Gilder: Posing a Rivalry of Forms." *Harvard Library Bulletin* n.s., 5, no. 2 (Summer 1994): 51–72.

Stein, Roger. "Picture and Text: The Literary World of Winslow Homer." In *Winslow Homer: A Symposium.* Washington, D.C.: Center for Advanced Study in the Visual Arts, National Gallery of Art, April 18, 1986.

"A Symposium of Wood Engravers." *Harper's New Monthly Magazine* 60 (February 1880): 442–53.

Tatham, David. *Winslow Homer Prints from "Harper's Weekly."* Exh. cat. Glens Falls, Rochester, and Hamilton, New York: Hyde Collection, Margaret Woodbury Strong Museum, and Gallery Association of New York State, 1979.

———. "Some Apprentice Lithographs of Winslow Homer— Ten Pictorial Title Pages for Sheet Music." *Old Time New England* 59 (April–June 1969): 86–104.

———. *Winslow Homer and the Illustrated Book.* Syracuse, New York: Syracuse University Press, 1992.

———. *Winslow Homer in the Adirondacks.* Syracuse, New York: Syracuse University Press, 1996.

Weitenkampf, L. H. D. *American Graphic Art.* New York: The Macmillan Company, 1924.

Wilmerding, John. "Winslow Homer's *Dad's Coming.*" In *In Honor of Paul Mellon, Collector and Benefactor,* ed. John Wilmerding, 389–401. Washington, D.C.: National Gallery of Art, 1986.

Wilson, Christopher Kent. "Winslow Homer's *Thanksgiving Day—Hanging Up the Musket.*" *American Art Journal* 17 (1986): 76–83.

———. "Marks of Honor and Death, *Sharpshooter* and the Peninsular Campaign of 1862." In Simpson et al., *Winslow Homer: Paintings of the Civil War,* 25–45.